2017 Innocents Database Exoneration Report

By Hans Sherrer

The Justice Institute
Seattle, Washington

2017 Innocents Database Exoneration Report

Copyright © 2018 by Hans Sherrer

Permission is granted to publish content in this report
with the sole proviso that credit for the source must be given.

Published by:
The Justice Institute
PO Box 66291
Seattle, WA 98166

Website: http://justicedenied.org
Email: contact@justicedenied.org

March 21, 2018

Trade Paperback ISBN: 1986769569
Trade Paperback ISBN: 978-1986769563

The map of the United States on the cover uses colors for each state to represent the total number of known exonerations for each state through 2017. The map was created with Carto.com.

The Justice Institute's logo that represents the snake of evil and injustice climbing up
to tilt the scales of justice, is in the lower right-hand corner of the cover.

Table of Contents

Introduction	1
Observations	3
Longest Time From Conviction To Judicial Exoneration	7
Longest Time From Conviction To Executive Exoneration	7
Longest Time From Commission Of Crime To Conviction	8
Table 1 — Known Exonerations By Year (U.S. & Int.)	10
Chart 1 — Exonerations By Year	10
Chart 2 — Exonerations By Year (Excluding 2017)	10
Table 2 — Number of Exonerated People By State	11
Map 1 — U.S. Map of Total Exonerations for each State	12
Table 3 — Number of Exonerated People By Jurisdiction (U.S.)	12
Table 4 — Number of Exonerated People By Sex/Type (U.S.)	12
Table 5 — Number of Exonerated People By Type of Crime (U.S.)	13
Chart 3 — Percentage of Exonerations by type of Crime (U.S.)	13
Table 6 — Number of Exonerated People by Race/Ethnicity (U.S.)	13
Table 7 — Number of Exonerated People By Primary Types of Exculpatory Evidence (U.S.)	14
Table 8 — Number of Exonerated People By Conviction Method (U.S.)	14
Table 9 — Number of Exonerated People Convicted After More Than One Trial (U.S.)	14
Table 10 — Number of State Prisoners Exonerated After Federal Habeas Granted (U.S.)	14
Table 11 — Number of Exonerated People Convicted By Primary Types of Prosecution Evidence* (U.S)	15
Table 12 — Number of Exonerated People By Method of Exoneration (U.S.)	15
Table 13 — Number of Exonerated Persons Involved In A Case With A Co-Defendant (U.S.)	15
Table 14 — Number of Exonerations Involving DNA Evidence By Year	16
Chart 4 — Exonerations Relying On DNA Evidence in the U.S. and Internationally	16
Chart 5 — Percentage of Exonerations based on DNA evidence – 1989-2006 (U.S.)	17
Table 15 — Number of Exonerations That Involved Conviction Integrity Unit (U.S.)	17
Table 16 — Number of Exonerations That Involved Original Investigation By Conviction Integrity Unit (U.S.)	17
Table 17 — Number of Exonerated People By Years In Custody (U.S.)	17
Table 18 — Average Years Exonerated Person Was In Custody Before Release (All types of cases)	18
Table 19 — Average Years Exonerated Person Was In Custody For Crime Of Violence (Violent crimes only)	18
Chart 6 — Average Years Exonerated Person Was In Custody For Crime Of Violence (Violent crimes only)	18
Table 20 — Average Years Exonerated Person Was In Custody Before Release (NON-violent crimes only)	19
Chart 7 — Avg Years Exonerated Person Was In Custody For Non-Violent Crime (U.S. & Int.)	19
Table 21 — Avg Years Exonerated Person Was In Custody Before Release (Homicide or Sexual Assault only)	19
Table 22 — Avg Years Exonerated Person Was In Custody (NON-Homicide or Sexual Assault crimes of violence)	19
Table 23 — Average Age Exonerated Person Was Taken Into Custody For Crime Of Violence (U.S. & Int.)	20
Table 24 — Average Age Exonerated Person Was Taken Into Custody For Non-Violent Crime (U.S. & Int.)	20
Table 25 — Average Age Of Person When Exonerated (ALL crimes) (U.S. & Int.)	20
Chart 8 — Average Age Of Person When Exonerated Of Violent Or Non-Violent Crime (U.S. & Int.)	20
Table 26 — Number of Exonerated People By County (12 or more) (U.S.)	21
Table 27 — Number of Exonerated People By Country – International Cases Only	22
Table 28 — Number of Exonerated People By Type of Crime (International)	24
Table 29 — Number of Exonerated People By Method of Exoneration (International)	24
Table 30 — Number of Exonerated Persons Involved In A Case With A Co-Defendant (International)	24
Map 2 — World Map Showing 120 Countries With Known Exoneration	25
21,587 People Exonerated In Massachusetts Due To Fraudulent Crime Lab Testing	25
Annie Dookhan's 8 Year Rampage Of Faking Scientific Evidence To Convict Innocent People Was Aided By Legal System	31
Germany's Cabinet Approves Pardon For More Than 50,000 Men Convicted Of Homosexual Crimes	33
German Parliament Approves Vindicating Males Of Homosexual Convictions	34
49,000 Men Posthumously Pardoned Of Homosexual Crimes In United Kingdom	36
165 Men Cleared Of Historical Homosexual Convictions in England and Wales	37

A question, correction, or suggestion regarding the Innocents Database can be emailed to:
innocents@justicedenied.org

Introduction

There were 21,831 known exonerations in the United States in 2017, and 99,219 known exonerations in other countries. That is a total of 121,050 known exonerations worldwide.

This is the third yearly report of information recorded in the Innocents Database through the last calendar year – 2017.[1] The Innocents Database is an ongoing independent non-profit project begun in February 1997.[2] The IDb is the world's only database that records every documentable exoneration in the United States and every other country.

The database includes references to 27,303 U.S. cases and 102,307 international cases concluded through December 31, 2017. A total of 129,610 cases from 120 countries.

The Innocents Database is online at **www.justicedenied.org/exonerations.htm**, and it can be accessed from Justice Denied's website at **www.justicedenied.org**. This Report is compiled from information available in the database online.[3]

Since the Innocents Database was founded there has been a continuing increase in the reporting of recent cases in accessible digital form. Finding and identifying contemporary cases is less challenging than 1995 cases, much less cases in 1985 or 1975.

Nevertheless, the 27,303 U.S. cases listed in the database through 2017 – 26,368 cases from 1989 to 2017 and 935 cases prior to 1989 – provide data that can be useful to make general observations and identify possible trends. 1989 is used as a quasi demarcation because the first DNA exoneration in the U.S. was in 1989. Internationally the first exoneration was in Canada in 1992.

The Report includes 30 tables of data, eight charts, and two maps. Many of the 30 tables include information about U.S. cases for both the years 1989 to 2017, and pre-1989, and several include information about international cases. The tables are:

- Table 1. Known Exonerations By Year (U.S. & Int.)
- Table 2. Number of Exonerated People By State
- Table 3. Number of Exonerated People By Jurisdiction (U.S.)
- Table 4. Number of Exonerated People By Sex/Type (U.S.)
- Table 5. Number of Exonerated People By Type of Crime (U.S.)
- Table 6. Number of Exonerated People by Race/Ethnicity (U.S.)
- Table 7. Number of Exonerated People By Primary Types of Exculpatory Evidence (U.S.)
- Table 8. Number of Exonerated People By Conviction Method (U.S.)
- Table 9. Number of Exonerated People Convicted After More Than One Trial (U.S.)
- Table 10. Number of State Prisoners Exonerated After Federal Habeas Granted (U.S.)
- Table 11. Number of Exonerated People Convicted By Primary Types of Prosecution Evidence (U.S.)
- Table 12. Number of Exonerated People By Method of Exoneration (U.S.)
- Table 13. Number of Exonerated Persons Involved In A Case With A Co-Defendant (U.S.)
- Table 14. Number of Exonerations Involving DNA Evidence By Year (U.S. & Int.)
- Table 15. Number of Exonerations That Involved Conviction Integrity Unit (U.S.)
- Table 16. Number of Exonerations Due To Original Investigation By Conviction Integrity Unit (U.S.)
- Table 17. Number of Exonerated People By Years In Custody (U.S.)

---

[1] This report includes cases that were concluded through December 31, 2017, and which were added to the database up to March 7, 2018. For an explanation of cases considered an exoneration for inclusion in the Innocents Database, see, Hans Sherrer, "An Exoneration Can Be Judicial Or By Executive Or Legislative Clemency," *Justice Denied*, Issue 59 (Spring 2015), available online at, http://justicedenied.org/wordpress/archives/2811. Summarized, an exoneration is when a convicted living or deceased person's presumption of innocence is restored by judicial, executive, or legislative action, or their conviction is recognized as a miscarriage of justice by either legislative or executive action based on evidence of their innocence.

[2] The Innocents Database was created and is maintained by Hans Sherrer, president of the Justice Institute, and publisher and editor of *Justice Denied: the magazine for the wrongly convicted*.

[3] The Innocents Database contains millions of bits of data. The database can be sorted and searched on over 100 fields online at, http://forejustice.org/exonerations.htm .

- Table 18. Average Years Exonerated Person Was In Custody Before Release (ALL crimes) (U.S. & Int.)
- Table 19. Avg. Years Exonerated Person Is In Custody Before Release (ALL violent crimes (U.S. & Int.)
- Table 20. Avg.Years Exonerated Person Is In Custody Before Release (NON-violent crimes (U.S. & Int.)
- Table 21. Average Years Exonerated Person Was In Custody Before Release (Homicide or Sexual Assault only) (U.S. & Int.)
- Table 22. Average Years Exonerated Person Was In Custody Before Release (Non-Homicide or Sexual Assault crimes of violence only) (U.S. & Int.)
- Table 23. Average Age Exonerated Person Was Taken Into Custody For Crime of Violence (U.S. & Int.)
- Table 24. Average Age Exonerated Person Was Taken Into Custody For Non-Violent Crime (U.S. & Int.)
- Table 25. Average Age Of Person When Exonerated (ALL crimes) (U.S. & Int.)[4]
- Table 26. Number of Exonerated People By County (12 or more) (U.S.)
- Table 27. Number of Exonerated People By Country – International Cases
- Table 28. Number of Exonerated People By Type of Crime (International)
- Table 29. Number of Exonerated People By Method of Exoneration (International)
- Table 30. Number of Exonerated Persons Involved In A Case With A Co-Defendant (International)

---

[4] This is the age when exonerated, so it includes people who were not sentenced before their exoneration, people who served all or part of their sentence on probation, and people who were exonerated after they completed serving their sentence.

Observations

In 2017 there were four unusual events that accounted for a significant number of exonerations both in the U.S. and internationally: 1) The posthumous pardoning of 49,000 men in England and Wales convicted of consensual homosexual related acts committed prior to 1967 that are no longer considered criminal; 2) The reporting that between 2012 and December 31, 2017, 165 men still alive in England and Wales had their convictions disregarded for consensual homosexual related acts committed prior to 1967 that are no longer considered criminal; 3) The legal vindication of 50,000 men in Germany – 45,000 posthumously and 5,000 still living – convicted of consensual homosexual related acts between 1945 and 1994 that are no longer considered criminal; and, 4) The Annie Dookhan drug evidence scandal at the Hinton State Laboratory in Massachusetts. (See articles published by *Justice Denied* about those events beginning on Report's page 26.

The following are observations regarding known exonerations in the United States in 2017. The data underlying these observations is in the tables in this report and the Innocents Database.

In 2017, there was an exoneration in 34 states and one in the U.S. territory of Guam.

In 2017, six states had 10 or more exonerations: Massachusetts (21,595); Ohio (42); Texas (38); Illinois (38); New York (20); Michigan (14).

Twelve counties had ten or more exonerations in 2017: Suffolk County, Massachusetts (15,571); Middlesex County, Massachusetts (2,169); Essex County, Massachusetts (1,067); Norfolk County, Massachusetts (965); Bristol County, Massachusetts (777); Plymouth County, Massachusetts (703); Barnstable County, Massachusetts (303); Cuyahoga County, Ohio (39); Cook County, Illinois (37); Dukes County, Massachusetts (24); Harris County, Texas (19); Nantucket County, Massachusetts (14).[5]

In 2017, about 89% of known exonerations were of men, and 11% were of women. That is almost identical to historical average for the last 40 years (89.5% men and 10.5% women).

In 2017, 99.5% of exonerations involved a case in which no crime was committed. That compares with the historical average for the last 40 years of 90%.

In 2017, 99.8% of exonerations were by way of dismissal of the charges. That compares with the historical average for the last 40 years of 91%.

In 2017, 26 exonerated people had one or more co-defendants also wrongly convicted. That compares with the historical average for the last 40 years of 17 per year.

In 2017, 99.3% of exonerations were of a drug related conviction. That compares with the historical average for the last 40 years of 87% drug related exonerations in a given year.

In 2017, there were two posthumously exonerations. That is comparable to the historical average for the last 40 years of three per year.

In 2017, 59 exonerated persons were in custody for 10 years or more, 40 for 20 years or more, 7 for 30 years or more, and one person spent more than 40 years in custody.

In 2017, 99.4% of exonerated people were convicted by a guilty or no-contest plea. That compares with the historical average for the last 40 years of 87%.

In 2017, there were 13 exonerations of a person convicted in federal court. That compares with the historical average for the last 40 years of 10 per year.

In 2017, there were 21 exonerations that involved a false confession by the exonerated person or a co-defendant. That compares with the historical average for the last 40 years of eight per year.

---

[5] 15,570 of the 21,587 Annie Dookhan tainted drug evidence cases dismissed by the Massachusetts Supreme Judicial Court on April 19, 2017 were in Suffolk County (pop. 746,039). Until exact data is obtained, the 6,017 non-Suffolk County cases are apportioned in the IDb based on the 2012 population of the other six counties affected by Annie Dookhan's conduct: Middlesex - 2,168 cases (pop. 1,537,149); Essex - 1,066 cases (pop. 755,970); Norfolk - 962 cases (pop. 682,078); Bristol - 777 cases (pop. 550,856); Plymouth - 703 cases (pop. 498,393); Barnstable - 303 cases (pop. 214,947); Dukes - 24 cases (pop. 16,834); Nantucket - 14 cases (pop. 10,241). (Population data from: www.us-places.com/Massachusetts/population-by-County.htm)

The average of 16 years spent in custody by people exonerated in 2017 of a homicide or sexual assault related crime was *four* times the average of 4 years spent in custody by an exonerated person who was convicted of any other type of crime.

In 2017 men exonerated of a homicide or sex assault related crime for which they were imprisoned were incarcerated for an average of 16-1/2 years; men convicted of all other crimes of violence were incarcerated for an average of 9-3/4 years; and men convicted of a non-violent crime were incarcerated for 2-1/3 years.

In 2017 women exonerated of a homicide or sex assault related crime for which they were imprisoned were incarcerated for an average of 9 years; women convicted of all over crimes of violence were incarcerated for an average of 1-3/4 years; and women convicted of a non-violent crime were incarcerated for 5 months.

In 2017, 30-1/2 was the average age of an exonerated man convicted for a crime of violence when taken into custody. That compares with the historical average for the last 40 years of 28-1/2.

In 2017, 37 was the average age of an exonerated man convicted for a non-violent crime when taken into custody. That is identical to the historical average for the last 40 years of 37.

In 2017, 27-1/2 was the average age of an exonerated woman convicted for a crime of violence when taken into custody. That compares with the historical average for the last 40 years of 32.

In 2017, 38 was the average age of an exonerated woman convicted for a non-violent crime when taken into custody. That is identical to the historical average for the last 40 years of 35.

In 2017, 45 was the average of a man when exonerated of their convicted crime.[6] That compares with the historical average for the last 40 years of 40-years-old. It is uncanny that 40 is also the same average age of a man when exonerated in all other countries during the last 40 years.

In 2017, 34-1/2 was the average of a woman when exonerated of their convicted crime.[7] That compares with the historical average for the last 40 years of 38-years-old.

In 2017, there were 11 exonerations primarily based on new DNA evidence. That is consistent with the average of 13 DNA exonerations yearly since the U.S.'s first DNA exoneration in 1989. Although they get a lot of media coverage, DNA exonerations are relatively uncommon. They have accounted for 1.4% — less than 1 out of very 70 exonerations since 1989.

In 2017, DNA evidence did not contribute to the exoneration of any women in 2017, although since 1989 it has contributed to the exoneration of 35 women.

In 2017, a conviction integrity unit in twelve jurisdictions was involved to some degree in the exoneration of 91 people: 38 in Cuyahoga County (Cleveland), Ohio; 27 in Cook County (Chicago), Illinois; 11 in Harris County (Houston) Texas; and 15 in eight other counties. Forty-nine of those 91 were pass-through cases – where the CIU effectively rubber-stamped an exoneration based on an investigation or evidence testing by others, or the retroactive application of a new court ruling that invalidated a conviction.

In 2017, a conviction integrity unit in six jurisdictions conducted the original investigation that resulted in the exoneration of 42 people: 36 in Cuyahoga County, Ohio; 2 in Kings County (Brooklyn), New York, and one each in four other counties. A CIU original investigation has resulted in only 13% of the exonerations that a CIU was involved in to some degree from 2008 to 2017 – and 60% of those were in Cuyahoga County and 31% were in Kings County, New York.[8] In contrast, 351 of the 354 exonerations aided by the Harris County CIU from 2014 to 2017 – 99.2% – were pass-through cases in which an exoneration was due to laboratory testing of evidence in drug cases that turned out not to be an illegal substance, or retroactive application of rulings in two cases in which the Texas Court of Criminal Appeals ruled the Texas statute relied on for the convictions was unconstitutional.[9]

---

[6] This is the age when exonerated, so it includes people who were not sentenced before their exoneration, people who served all or part of their sentence on probation, and people who were incarcerated.
[7] *Id.*
[8] DA Thompson died of cancer at the age of 50 on October 9, 2016. It is unknown at this time if his predecessor will support the CRU as a dynamic mechanism to ferret out unreliable convictions, or revert to the approach of Thompson's predecessor Charles Hynes., that the CRU was effectively only a public relations prop.
[9] The two statutes involved online solicitation of a minor, and photographing people in public without consent.

In 2017, one state prisoners was exonerated after their federal habeas corpus petition was granted. That is less than the average of three to four per year since enactment of the Anti-terrorism and Effective Death Penalty Act of 1996.[10] The difficulty of a state prisoner to prevail in federal court is emphasized by the small number of exonerations contrasted with the thousands of state prisoner habeas petitions filed annually in U.S. District Courts.[11] The reality of that situation is opposite of the widely believed folklore a state prisoner can expect to get a fairer shake in federal court than their state's courts.[12] The 2016 Innocents Database Exoneration Report included an article whose title perfectly sums up the situation: *Federal Court Is The Death Zone For Innocent State Prisoners.*" The article can be read at, www.justicedenied.org/wordpress/archives/3511 .

In the U.S. there are over a million felony convictions yearly in state courts, and more than 125,000 convictions in federal courts, so even given only a 2% wrongful conviction rate – and there are estimates the actual rate is 10% or more – there would be more than 22,000 wrongful convictions per year.[13] What is unknown – and for the foreseeable future it will remain unknown – is exactly how many innocent people have had their wrongful conviction(s) overturned. Also unknown is the infinitely larger number of innocent people – possibly totaling over a million – who have not, and never will have their wrongful conviction(s) overturned: those people will forever be officially branded as a criminal for a crime committed by another person, or that may not have even occurred. Thus, the known exonerations are an incomplete representation of the actual number of wrongly convicted persons.

The inadequacy of current data regarding wrongful convictions is illustrated by the fact that even though far more Caucasians are convicted than any other "racial" group, 49% of the exonerations in 2017 was of a Black when the person's racial identity is known.

The following are observations regarding known exonerations in countries other than the United States in 2017. The data underlying these observations is in the tables in this report and the Innocents Database.

In 2017, there was an identifiable exoneration in 35 countries. That is comparable to the 41 countries with a known exoneration in 2016 and the 39 in 2015.

In 2017, four countries had 10 or more known exonerations: Germany (50,000); United Kingdom (England) (49,046); India (43); and, Australia (10).

In 2017, 99.974% of exonerations were of a man, and .026% were of a woman. With the exception of 2017, during which a large number of men were exonerated for a consensual homosexual act that is no longer illegal, the historical average for the last 40 years is 87% men and 13% women.

In 2017, 99.9% of exonerations involved a case in which no crime was committed.

In 2017, 49.4% of exonerations were by way of a pardon for a criminal conviction for consensual homosexual activity that is no longer considered criminal. 50.4% of exonerations by way of legislation to eliminate a criminal conviction for consensual homosexual activity that is no longer considered criminal.

In 2017, 105 exonerated people had one of more co-defendants also wrongly convicted.

In 2017, 99.85% of exonerations were of a non-violent related conviction.

In 2017, there were 94,0001 posthumous exonerations internationally.

In 2017, one person was exonerated after more than 20 years of imprisonment, and nine were exonerated after

---

[10] Also known as AEDPA, Pub. L. No. 104-132, 110 Stat. 1214. Signed into law by President Clinton on April 24, 1996.
[11] See, Judicial Facts and Figures 2015, Table 4.6. "U.S. District Courts – Prisoner Petition Filed, by Nature of Suit," USCourts.gov. Available online at, http://www.uscourts.gov/sites/default/files/data_tables/jff_4.6_0930.2016.pdf. (Last visited March 20, 2018) 2016 is the most recent year that the statistics are available.
[12] See the article by Hans Sherrer, *"Federal Court Is The Death Zone For Innocent State Prisoners,"* published by *Justice Denied* on February 16, 2017. Available online at, http://justicedenied.org/wordpress/archives/3511 .
[13] 967,853 defendants were convicted in federal court during the seven years 2010 to 2016 – an average of 138,264 per year. See, U.S. Attorneys' Statistical Reports available online at, http://www.justice.gov/usao/resources/annual-statistical-reports (Last visited March 20, 2018). There were 1,132,290 felony convictions in state courts in 2006, the latest year for which the data is available from the Bureau of Justice Statistics. See, Sean Rosenmerkel, Matthew Durose and Donald Farole, Jr., Ph.D.; "Felony Sentences in State Courts, 2006 – Statistical Tables," *Bureau of Justice Statistics*, December 2009, NCJ 226846. Available online at, http://www.bjs.gov/content/pub/pdf/fssc06st.pdf (Last viewed March 17, 2018).

ten years of imprisonment.

In 2017, men exonerated of a homicide or sex assault related crime for which they were imprisoned were incarcerated for an average of 5-2/3 years; men convicted of all over crimes of violence were incarcerated for an average of 2 years; and men convicted of a non-violent crime were incarcerated for 1-1/2 years.

In 2017, women exonerated of a homicide or sex assault related crime for which they were imprisoned were incarcerated for an average of 3-1/2 years; women convicted of all over crimes of violence were incarcerated for an average of 1-1/4 years; and women convicted of a non-violent crime were incarcerated for about 2 months.

In 2017, 42-1/2 was the average age of an exonerated man convicted for a crime of violence when taken into custody. That compares with the historical average for the last 40 years of 40.

In 2017, 37 was the average age of an exonerated man convicted for a non-violent crime when taken into custody. That compares with the historical average for the last 40 years of 40.

In 2017, 43 was the average age of an exonerated woman convicted for a crime of violence when taken into custody. That compares with the historical average for the last 40 years of 36.

In 2017, 40 was the average age of an exonerated woman convicted for a non-violent crime when taken into custody. That compares with the historical average for the last 40 years of 34.

In 2017, 41 was the average of a man when exonerated of his convicted crime.[14] That compares with the historical average for the last 40 years of 40 years old. It is uncanny that 40 is also the same average age of a man when exonerated in the U.S. during the last 40 years.

In 2017, 42-1/2 was the average of a woman when exonerated of their convicted crime.[15] That compares with the historical average for the last 40 years of 35 years old. The 40 year average for women in the U.S. is 38.

In 2017, there were 2 exonerations primarily based on new DNA evidence. That is consistent with the average of about 2 DNA exonerations yearly since the first international DNA exoneration in 1992. All DNA exonerations internationally have been of a male.

---

[14] This is the age when exonerated, so it includes people who were not sentenced before their exoneration, people who served all or part of their sentence on probation, and people who were incarcerated.

[15] *Id.*

The following are three notable U.S. 2017 exoneration cases: the longest time from conviction to a judicial exoneration; the longest time from conviction to an executive (pardon) exoneration; and the longest time from an exonerated person's conviction and the commission of the crime.

Longest Time From Conviction To Judicial Exoneration

41 years 3 months
Ledura Watkins
Convicted in 1976. Exonerated in 2017.
Wayne County, Michigan

Ledura Watkins was convicted on March 16, 1976 of first-degree murder in the death of 25-year-old Yvette Ingram during a robbery at her home in Detroit, Michigan on September 6, 1975. Watkins was arrested on October 22, 1975 and charged with first-degree murder, based on the police statement by Travis Herndon that Watkins committed the robbery and murder. Watkins had been arrested for an unrelated robbery.

During Watkins' trial the prosecution's case was based on testimony of Herndon, and a crime lab technician's testimony that a single hair recovered form the crime scene more likely than not matched Watkins' hair. There was no other physical, forensic, eyewitness or confession evidence linking him to the crime.

After his conviction by the jury Watkins was sentenced to life in prison without parole.

The Michigan Court of Appeals affirmed his conviction and sentence.

In 1980 and 1981 Herndon recanted his trial testimony when he testified during an unsuccessful post-conviction appeal by Watkins. Herndon testified his trial testimony was false, and Watkins wasn't involved in the robbery and Ingram's murder.

Decades later the FBI acknowledged hair comparison was unreliable to match a person to a crime scene.

Watkins filed a post-conviction petition for a new trial in 2017 that was based on the FBI's repudiation of the reliability of hair analysis; Herndon's recantation; and police and laboratory reports prosecutors hadn't disclosed to Watkins' trial lawyer.

The Wayne County District Attorney's Office acknowledged that Watkins' conviction was unreliable under the new FBI standard regarding hair comparison, and did not oppose his petition. On June 15, 2017 the motion by the Wayne County District Attorney to dismiss the charges against Watkins was granted, and he was released from custody.

Longest Time From Conviction To Executive Exoneration

37 years 11 months
Craig Richard Coley
Convicted in 1980. Exonerated in 2017.
Ventura County, California

Craig Richard Coley was convicted on January 3, 1980 of two counts of first-degree murder in the death of 24-year-old Rhonda Wicht, who he had been dating for two years, and her 4-year-old son Donald, in Simi Valley, California in November 1978.

It was Coley's second trial. In April 1979 his first trial ended with a hung jury: after four weeks of deliberations the jury was deadlocked at a 10 to 2 vote for a guilt verdict.

The prosecution's case against Craig Coley was based on circumstantial evidence. There was no physical, eyewitness or confession evidence linking Coley to the crime. The case against him was so weak that during his trial *The Simi Valley Mirror* – the local newspaper – ran a front-page story titled: "Coley Truly Appears to Be Wrong Man." *The Mirror's* publisher, James A. Whitehead, published an editorial that attacked the Simi Valley police for its investigation of the case and stated: "*The Mirror* is firmly convinced that Glen Watkins should be arrested as he is definitely a suspect of committing murder in the first-degree ..."[16]

After his conviction by a jury Coley was sentenced to life in prison without parole.

Coley's case was reopened in October 2016 by Simi Valley Police Chief David Livingstone after a retired detective expressed doubts about Coley's guilty. Investigators later found a key piece of prosecution evidence did not match Coley's DNA, but it did contain the DNA of unidentified persons.

On November 22, 2017 California Governor Jerry Brown pardoned Craig Coley on the basis the Simi County Police Department and the Ventura County District Attorney's Office had determined he did not commit the crime, and he had been wrongly convicted. Gov. Brown ordered Coley's immediate release from prison.

On Nov. 22 Ventura County District Attorney Gregory D. Totten and Police Chief Livingstone released a joint statement that the murder case was reopened to pursue finding the real killer or killers of Rhonda and Donald.

Coley filed a wrongful imprisonment claim with the California Victim Compensation Board. On February 15, 2018 the VCB voted unanimously to award Coley compensation of $140 per day for 13,991 days (38.33 yrs) of incarceration: a total of $1,958,740. It was the largest amount awarded by the VCB in a wrongful imprisonment case.

Longest Time From Commission Of Crime To Conviction

3-1/2 years
Michael Escort
Crime occurred in 1989. Convicted in 2014. Exonerated in 2017.
Cook County, Illinois

Murder
60 yrs in prison

Michael Escort was convicted in 2014 of murdering 33-year-old Mary Smith in Chicago, Illinois on October 3, 1989. Smith was a drug user who was working as a prostitute. She was beaten and strangled, and her death was unsolved for more than a decade.

In July 2011 the Chicago Police Department cold case unit submitted two vaginal swab sticks, two rectal swab sticks, and two oral swab sticks collected from Smith for DNA analysis by Cellmark Forensics laboratory. The tests resulted in identification of DNA from a number of different sources, but only two in which enough DNA was recovered to identify a profile: Those were identified as "Unknown male number 1" and "Unknown male number 2." The Illinois State Police crime lab uploaded the profiles to the FBI's national CODIS DNA database. A match resulted for "Unknown male number 1", who was identified as Michael Escort.

At the time Escort was in prison in Illinois for unrelated convictions of aggravated criminal sexual assault and aggravated kidnapping. Escort agreed to have additional DNA samples taken from his cheek and lower lip. Further testing identified that Escort's DNA matched sperm recovered from the vaginal swabs. However, his DNA did not match a sample from the semen stain on Smith's pants, and his DNA did not match sperm recovered from Smith's pantyhose, so he was excluded as the source of that DNA.

Escort denied having anything to do with Smith's murder. He was "arrested" for Smith's murder on December 6, 2012 – although he was already in prison – and on January 3, 2013 he was indicted by a grand jury with murder and felony murder for which the predicate felony was criminal sexual assault.

The trial judge granted – over Escort's objection – the prosecution's pre-trial motion to introduce admission of "bad character" evidence that in 1991 he had been convicted in an unrelated case of aggravated criminal sexual

---

[16] "He spent 39 years behind bars for two murders he didn't commit. Gov. Jerry Brown just pardoned him," By Alene Tchekmedyian (Reporter), *Los Angeles Times*, November 23, 2017. Online at, http://www.latimes.com/local/lanow/la-me-ln-jerry-brown-pardon-20171122-htmlstory.html .

assault of his then girlfriend's 13-year-old daughter. The judge ruled that the probative value of the "bad character" evidence outweighed its prejudicial impact.

During Escort's trial the State's case was based on the DNA evidence that proved Smith – who was working as a street prostitute – had sex with Escort sometime within 72 hours of her death, and the "bad character" evidence of his 1991 conviction. It was brought out during cross-examination of the State's witnesses that the DNA of an undetermined number of other men was also identified from the sperm recovered from Smith, and that Escort's DNA didn't match the sperm found on her pants and pantyhose, which would be likely places her killer would have deposited his sperm.

At the conclusion of the State's case Escort's lawyer made a motion for a directed verdict, "arguing that the State's evidence proved only that he had sexual relations with the victim, but not that he had murdered her. The trial court denied the defendant's motion, and the defendant then rested without introducing any evidence."[17]

After the jury found Escort guilty, the judge denied his motion for a verdict of acquittal. Escort was subsequently sentenced to 60 years imprisonment.

Escort appealed. On November 22, 2017 the Illinois Appellate Court, First District unanimously reversed Escort's convictions on the basis the prosecution failed to introduce sufficient evidence he committed Smith's murder. The Court's ruling stated: "¶ 21 Distilled to its finest, the State's evidence could reasonably support only a determination that the defendant had sexual relations with the victim at some time during the 72-hour period prior to her death. It would be pure speculation to conclude that the defendant and the victim had sexual relations shortly before her death or that he was the last person to see the victim alive. However, guilt may not rest on speculation. [] ¶ 22 Our examination of the record in this case leads us to conclude that the evidence introduced by the State was so weak as to create a reasonable doubt on the issue of whether the defendant committed the murder of Mary Smith. Consequently, we reverse the defendant's conviction and sentence ..."[18]

Escort's retrial was barred by double-jeopardy, since the court's ruling was based on insufficient prosecution evidence presented during his trial. The charges were dismissed and Escort was released from prison on December 1, 2017.

---

[17] *State of Illinois v. Michael Escort*, 2017 IL App (1st) 151247 (Ill. Appellate Ct., 1st Dist., 11-22-2017)
[18] *Id.*

Table 1 — Known Exonerations By Year (U.S. & Int.)				
Year	USA	Posthumous	International	Posthumous
2017	21,831	2	99,219	94,001
2016	489	0	505	2
2015	730	4	243	2
2014	520	4	240	1
2013	210	4	225	0
2012	154	0	153	2
2011	131	2	160	1
2010	339	0	97	0
2009	157	3	156	3
2008	138	0	163	0
2007	143	28	172	8
2006	179	80	115	3
2005	87	0	107	1
2004	95	0	139	0
2003	130	2	81	3
2002	91	1	50	2
2001	109	1	51	0
2000	258	2	33	0
1999	62	0	27	0
1998	50	0	34	4
1997	57	0	15	0
1996	62	1	8	0
1995	85	0	20	0
1994	44	0	10	0
1993	48	0	9	0
1992	45	0	18	0
1991	50	0	13	0
1990	39	0	6	0
1989	35	1	17	0
1989-2017 total	26,368	135	102,086	94,033
<1989 total	935	27	221	34
Total	27,303	162	102,307	94,067

Chart 1

Exonerations By Year (U.S. & International)

Chart 2

Exonerations By Year (U.S. & International) (Excluding 2017)

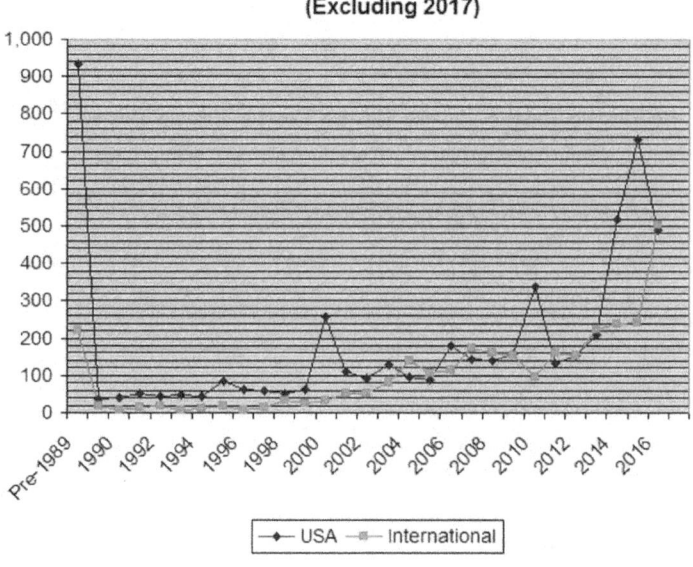

Table 2 — Number of Exonerated People By State														
State/Territory	2017	2016	2015	2014	2013	2012	2011	2010	2009	2008	10 yr total	1989-2016	Pre-1989	Total
Alabama	0	0	5	1	3	2	2	0	1	0	14	40	18	58
Alaska	0	0	6	1	0	1	0	0	0	0	8	9	4	13
American Samoa	0	0	0	1	0	0	0	0	0	0	1	1	0	1
Arizona	2	1	1	1	1	4	0	3	1	1	15	33	1	34
Arkansas	1	2	3	1	1	0	1	3	0	1	13	17	8	25
California	8	13	11	12	9	13	12	7	13	11	109	419	83	502
Colorado	1	3	2	4	0	1	2	2	0	0	15	18	2	20
Connecticut	1	1	6	0	10	1	0	1	3	1	24	39	8	47
Delaware	1	1	5	0	0	0	0	0	0	0	7	7	0	7
Dist. of Columbia	1	1	2	3	1	5	1	0	3	0	17	25	13	38
Florida	4	4	12	4	3	3	1	5	3	5	44	122	46	168
Georgia	4	4	4	0	6	1	1	1	4	3	28	51	21	72
Guam	1	0	2	0	1	0	0	0	1	0	5	5	0	5
Hawaii	0	0	0	2	1	0	1	0	0	0	4	7	0	7
Idaho	0	3	0	0	0	1	0	0	0	0	4	6	3	9
Illinois	38	19	25	18	19	14	12	5	10	12	172	279	41	320
Indiana	4	4	6	0	1	5	0	1	2	5	28	47	8	55
Iowa	1	4	8	4	2	2	2	0	1	0	24	35	2	37
Kansas	1	5	3	2	1	0	1	0	1	0	14	19	3	22
Kentucky	3	0	1	2	0	1	1	1	1	4	14	23	6	29
Louisiana	8	3	3	3	1	2	4	4	0	1	29	69	24	93
Maine	1	1	1	1	0	0	1	0	1	0	6	7	4	11
Maryland	9	2	1	3	2	1	1	2	0	2	23	43	14	57
Massachusetts	21,595	4	4	2	5	6	3	7	1	4	21,631	21,681	75	21,756
Michigan	14	5	2	18	7	7	1	27	20	9	110	156	64	220
Minnesota	1	3	5	1	2	0	2	3	0	1	18	28	6	34
Mississippi	4	1	1	0	0	0	3	6	3	4	22	31	8	39
Missouri	2	2	2	2	5	2	2	5	3	3	28	60	13	73
Montana	4	3	2	1	0	0	0	0	1	1	12	95	0	95
Nebraska	1	1	2	1	0	0	0	1	5	1	12	17	2	19
Nevada	3	5	3	1	0	0	1	0	1	0	14	28	6	34
New Hampshire	0	0	2	1	1	0	1	0	2	0	7	8	0	8
New Jersey	4	6	6	5	2	1	0	173	2	0	199	218	37	255
New Mexico	0	0	1	4	1	0	0	0	1	1	8	13	7	20
New York	20	34	41	34	21	29	15	15	14	14	237	390	188	578
North Carolina	0	9	21	5	2	6	3	5	2	3	56	76	26	102
North Dakota	0	1	0	0	0	0	1	0	0	1	3	7	0	7
Ohio	42	10	6	10	2	2	7	9	4	17	109	164	37	201
Oklahoma	0	5	2	3	1	3	9	18	4	1	46	66	10	76
Oregon	2	16	2	4	1	3	2	4	2	0	36	49	6	55
Pennsylvania	2	151	403	112	54	2	6	2	2	0	734	833	25	858
Puerto Rico	0	3	0	0	0	1	0	0	1	1	6	6	0	6
Rhode Island	0	0	0	1	0	1	2	1	0	0	5	9	0	9
South Carolina	0	2	1	2	3	1	1	1	2	0	13	19	38	57
South Dakota	0	0	1	0	0	0	0	0	0	1	2	7	0	7
Tennessee	1	4	6	3	2	2	2	1	2	1	24	41	3	44
Texas	38	134	75	229	12	16	18	15	18	15	570	688	27	725
Utah	5	1	1	3	0	1	1	0	1	0	13	24	2	26
Vermont	0	0	1	0	2	0	0	0	0	0	3	4	2	6
Virgin Islands	0	0	0	0	0	0	0	0	0	2	2	2	0	2
Virginia	1	12	11	3	5	3	4	1	5	3	48	78	14	92
Washington	0	2	9	3	12	5	2	5	4	2	44	96	10	106
West Virginia	0	1	0	2	0	0	0	1	2	4	10	19	3	22
Wisconsin	2	2	9	5	4	2	1	4	8	2	39	72	7	79
Wyoming	0	1	0	1	2	2	1	0	0	0	7	7	0	7
U.S. Military	1	0	4	1	2	2	0	0	2	0	12	45	10	55
Totals	21,831	489	730	520	210	154	131	339	157	137	24,698	26,368	935	27,303

Map 1 — U.S. Map of Total Exonerations for each State (See Table 2's Total column for data.)

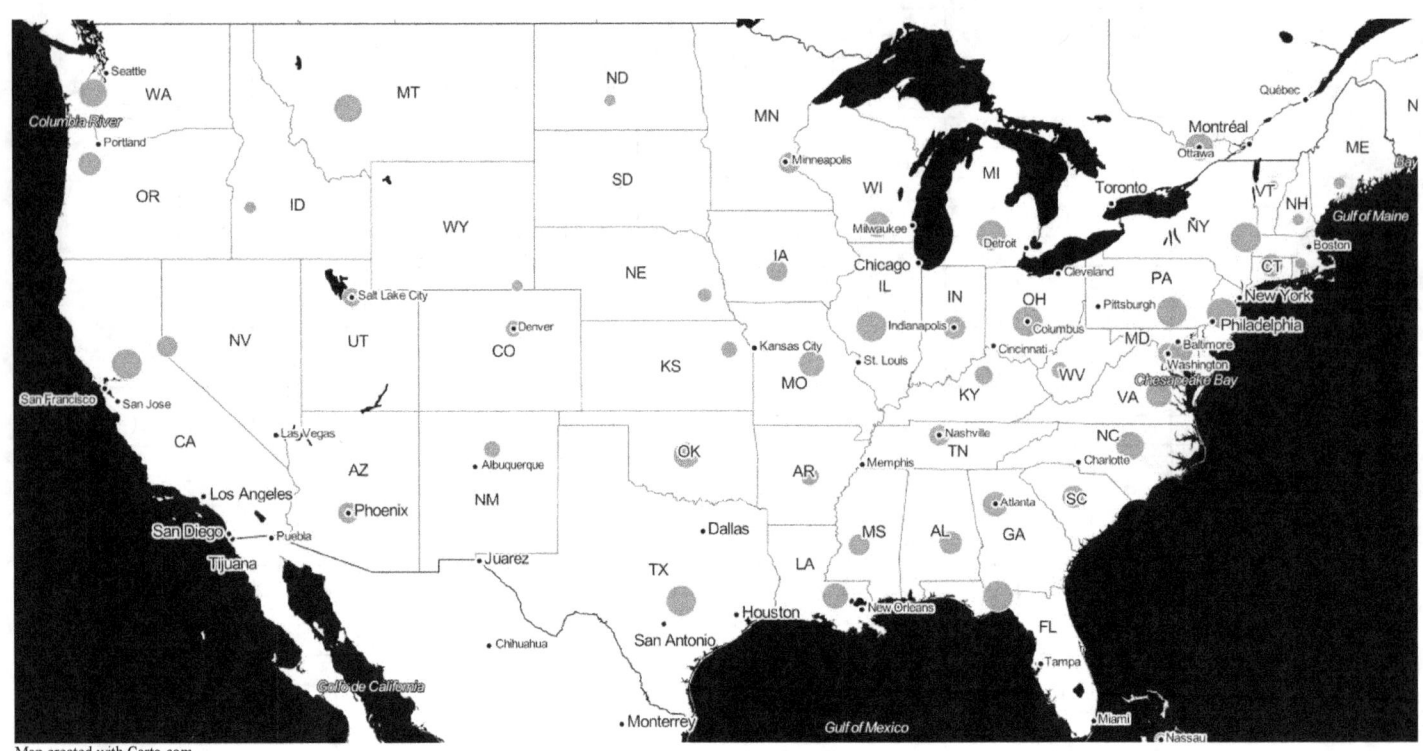

Map created with Carto.com.

Table 3 — Number of Exonerated People By Jurisdiction (U.S.)

Jurisdiction	2017	2016	2015	2014	2013	2012	2011	2010	2009	2008	10 yr total	1989-2017	Pre-1989	Total
State case	21,818	470	699	492	191	135	117	318	139	110	24,489	25,995	795	26,790
Federal case	13	19	31	28	19	19	14	21	18	28	210	373	140	513
Total	21,831	489	730	520	210	154	131	339	157	138	24,699	26,368	935	27,303

Table 4 — Number of Exonerated People By Sex/Type (U.S.)

Type	2017	2016	2015	2014	2013	2012	2011	2010	2009	2008	10 yr total	1989-2017	Pre-1989	Total
Male	218	307	295	209	137	134	118	217	137	123	1895	3221	844	4065
Female	26	39	40	38	20	19	12	24	20	15	253	402	71	473
Business	0	0	1	1	0	1	1	1	0	0	5	6	4	10
Unknown	21,587	143	394	272	53	0	0	97	0	0	22,546	22,739	16	22,755
Total	21,831	489	730	520	210	154	131	339	157	138	24,699	26,368	935	27,303

Table 5 — Number of Exonerated People By Type of Crime (U.S.)														
Type	2017	2016	2015	2014	2013	2012	2011	2010	2009	2008	10 yr total	1989-2017	Pre-1989	Total
Homicide	59	61	80	57	49	39	35	40	54	33	507	1,007	430	1,437
Homicide/Sex	2	7	3	2	2	7	6	5	4	3	41	92	5	97
Sexual Assault/Rape/Indecent Assault	13	8	12	16	20	20	16	19	23	21	168	397	42	439
Child Sex Assault/Abuse	19	26	12	9	9	12	11	12	10	12	132	245	3	248
Robbery/Theft/Burglary/Extortion	9	7	15	11	10	9	12	11	12	14	110	217	116	333
Assault	9	9	21	11	2	6	5	6	5	4	78	134	8	142
Drug	21,672	257	472	337	73	19	13	201	21	17	23,082	23,399	17	23,415
Fraud/Forgery/Embezzlement/Bribery	6	10	18	10	16	9	5	10	9	11	104	154	45	199
Child Abuse/Assault	2	3	1	4	1	0	0	1	1	0	13	20	0	20
Violent Other	5	12	21	17	12	8	2	12	6	12	107	174	57	231
Non-violent Other	35	89	75	46	16	25	26	22	12	11	357	529	212	741
Total	21,831	489	730	520	210	154	131	339	157	138	24,699	26,368	935	27,303

Chart 3

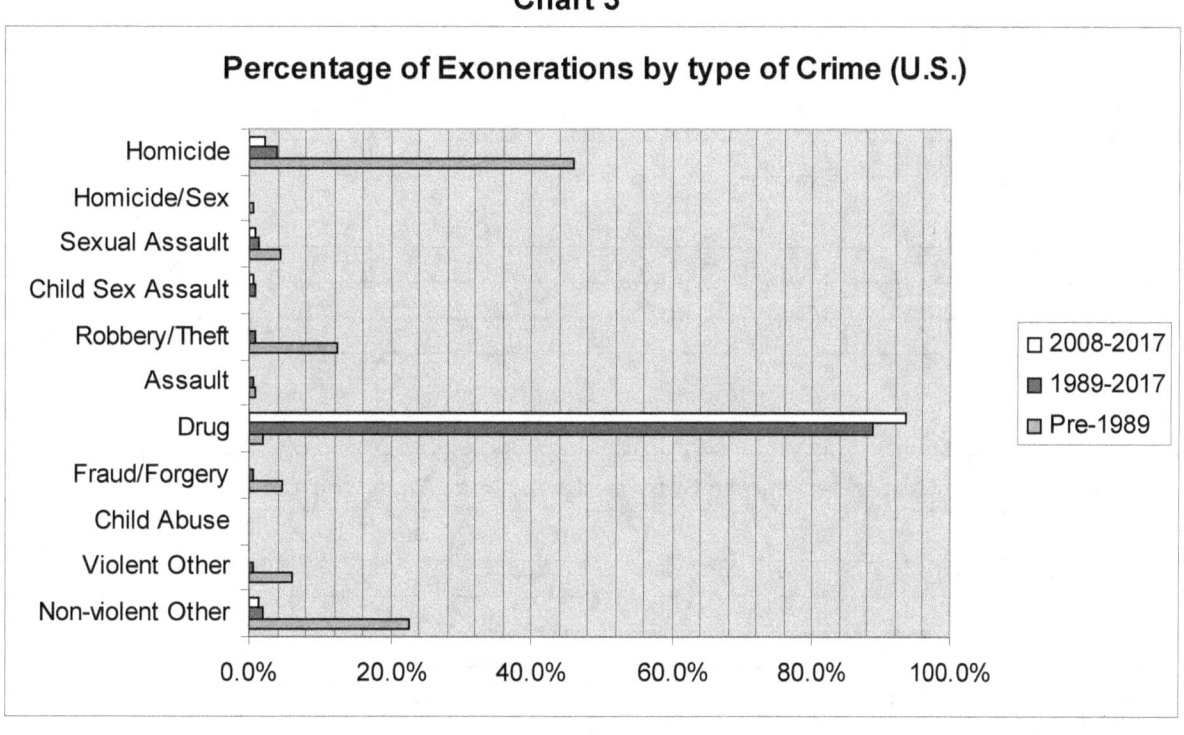

Percentage of Exonerations by type of Crime (U.S.)

Table 6 — Number of Exonerated People by Race/Ethnicity (U.S.)														
Type	2017	2016	2015	2014	2013	2012	2011	2010	2009	2008	10 yr total	1989-2017	Pre-1989	Total
White	59	78	98	79	56	56	45	47	54	48	620	1233	459	1692
Black	82	104	110	85	56	53	51	57	52	42	692	1214	186	1400
Hispanic	18	23	30	18	9	17	8	8	7	9	147	289	25	314
Asian	3	2	4	2	2	0	1	1	1	0	16	22	6	28
Native American	0	1	8	0	1	0	0	1	0	0	11	16	2	18
Middle eastern roots	0	1	0	1	0	0	0	0	0	0	2	2	0	2
Black/Asian	0	0	0	0	0	0	0	0	0	0	0	1	0	1
Indian (India)	4	0	0	0	0	0	0	0	0	0	4	4	0	4
Other	0	1	2	4	0	0	1	1	1	0	10	15	0	15
Unidentified	21,665	279	478	331	86	28	25	224	42	39	23,197	23,576	257	23,833
Total	21,831	489	730	520	210	154	131	339	157	138	24,699	26,368	935	27,303

Table 7 — Number of Exonerated People By Primary Types of Exculpatory Evidence* (U.S.)														
Type	2017	2016	2015	2014	2013	2012	2011	2010	2009	2008	10 yr total	1989-2017	Pre-1989	Total
No crime occurred	21,721	361	594	388	107	46	33	221	44	43	23,558	24,035	260	24,295
Insufficient evidence	21,626	96	122	37	23	23	21	27	23	31	22,029	22,135	198	22,333
New forensic evidence (DNA & other)	21,652	112	89	238	23	32	29	29	30	28	22,262	22,457	27	22,484
Prosecution concealment of evidence	21,667	195	427	125	77	13	17	200	36	7	22,764	23,095	55	23,150
Prosecution fabricated evidence	21,651	167	407	115	60	1	8	191	4	2	22,606	22,839	12	22,851
New witness evidence	17	23	18	9	11	6	3	7	4	3	101	161	65	226
Recantation by accuser	20	38	14	15	4	6	17	10	9	4	137	195	40	235
New DNA evidence**	11	17	12	9	11	19	22	18	22	18	159	374	0	374
Confession by perpetrator	4	9	5	6	7	5	3	4	2	6	51	124	99	223
CCTV, Electronic, or Photographic evidence	5	8	13	5	4	3	3	2	0	1	44	55	0	55

* More than one can apply to a particular case
** Does not include cases where DNA was contributory evidence

Table 8 — Number of Exonerated People By Conviction Method (U.S.)														
Type	2017	2016	2015	2014	2013	2012	2011	2010	2009	2008	10 yr total	1989-2017	Pre-1989	Total
Jury trial	117	147	174	107	106	89	82	99	97	87	1105	1848	554	2402
Judge (Bench trial)	15	33	63	30	11	11	12	11	12	11	209	263	93	356
Guilty Plea	21,690	302	489	344	74	25	13	187	10	21	23,155	23,272	23	23,295
Alford Plea	7	7	4	4	0	3	1	5	1	2	34	50	2	52
Unidentified	2	0	0	35	19	26	23	37	37	17	196	935	263	1198
Total	21,831	489	730	520	210	154	131	339	157	138	24,669	26,368	935	27,303

Table 9 — Number of Exonerated People Convicted After More Than One Trial (U.S.)														
Type	2017	2016	2015	2014	2013	2012	2011	2010	2009	2008	10 yr total	1989-2017	Pre-1989	Total
2 trials	13	13	23	7	7	3	4	4	6	4	84	181	82	263
3 trials	3	1	1	2	3	3	1	1	1	1	17	29	18	47
4 trials	0	2	0	1	1	0	0	0	0	0	4	6	1	7
5 trials	1	0	0	0	0	0	0	0	0	0	1	3	3	6
Total	17	16	24	10	11	6	5	5	7	5	106	219	104	323

Table 10 — Number of State Prisoners Exonerated After Federal Habeas Granted (U.S.)														
Year	2017	2016	2015	2014	2013	2012	2011	2010	2009	2008	10 yr total	1989-2017	Pre-1989	Total
Number	1	8	7	3	4	2	5	4	6	4	44	98	39	137

Table 11 — Number of Exonerated People Convicted By Primary Types of Prosecution Evidence* (U.S)														
Type	2017	2016	2015	2014	2013	2012	2011	2010	2009	2008	10 yr total	1989-2017	Pre-1989	Total
Eyewitness error	51	28	40	40	34	25	28	31	26	51	354	712	224	936
Victim ID error	28	41	34	24	22	22	18	24	13	18	244	407	66	473
Informant evidence	6	18	14	10	7	2	11	8	11	3	90	176	51	227
Expert witness	21,605	23	14	5	6	12	8	11	10	12	21,706	21,826	16	21,842
Judge's Errors	45	68	96	37	23	24	12	21	20	22	368	466	144	610
Police Misconduct/Perjury	95	196	429	134	72	20	22	202	22	9	1201	1519	68	1587
Prosecutor Misconduct	20	38	34	25	20	14	12	13	14	8	198	381	75	456
False Confession	21	13	28	22	10	11	11	17	13	26	172	315	75	390
Co-defendant falsely confessed (Defendant didn't confess)	0	0	1	0	0	0	1	0	0		02	59	9	68
Concealed evidence	76	188	424	125	77	14	4	183	16	6	1113	1476	65	1541
Circumstantial evidence	12	40	42	35	12	7	8	10	10	3	179	236	160	396
Drug analysis (erroneous)	21,607	82	53	215	1	1	0	0	1	0	21,960	21,961	0	21,961

* More than one can apply to a particular case

Table 12 — Number of Exonerated People By Method of Exoneration (U.S.)														
Type	2017	2016	2015	2014	2013	2012	2011	2010	2009	2008	10 yr total	1989-2017	Pre-1989	Total
Acquitted by Court	37	114	129	92	38	28	27	28	25	10	528	666	230	896
Acquitted after Retrial	9	15	20	9	11	8	5	10	5	5	97	213	75	288
Charges dismissed	21,782	358	577	416	157	117	97	299	117	120	24,040	25,144	458	25,602
Pardoned	3	2	4	2	4	1	2	2	10	3	33	202	136	338
Coram Nobis	0	0	0	1	0	0	0	0	0	0	1	8	9	17
Posthumous	2	0	4	4	4	0	2	0	3	0	19	135	27	162
Total	21,831	489	730	520	210	154	131	339	157	138	24,699	26,368	935	27,303

Table 13 — Number of Exonerated Persons Involved In A Case With A Co-Defendant (U.S.)														
Type	2017	2016	2015	2014	2013	2012	2011	2010	2009	2008	10 yr total	1989-2017	Pre-1989	Total
2 Co-defendants	12	22	15	29	8	10	12	10	23	14	155	331	96	427
3 Co-defendants	0	7	12	3	7	6	4	6	4	4	53	90	38	128
4 Co-defendants	9	6	8	3	8	4	1	0	2	0	41	72	21	93
5 Co-defendants	5	0	3	0	8	3	6	0	0	0	25	44	22	66
6 Co-defendants	0	0	0	0	0	0	0	0	5	1	6	6	12	18
7 Co-defendants	0	1	0	3	3	0	0	0	0	0	7	14	14	28
9 Co-defendants	0	0	9	0	3	0	0	0	0	0	12	12	15	27
10 Co-defendants	0	0	10	0	0	0	0	0	0	0	10	10	10	20
12 Co-defendants	0	0	0	0	0	0	0	0	0	0	0	18	0	18
14 Co-defendants	0	0	0	0	0	0	0	0	0	0	0	0	14	14
16 Co-defendants	0	0	0	0	0	0	0	0	0	0	0	0	16	16
17 Co-defendants	0	0	0	0	0	0	0	0	0	0	0	0	17	17
24 Co-defendants	0	0	0	0	0	0	0	0	0	0	0	0	48	48
28 Co-defendants	0	0	0	0	0	0	0	0	0	28	28	28	0	28
Total	26	36	57	38	37	23	23	16	34	19	309	607	341	948

Table 14 — Number of Exonerations Involving DNA Evidence By Year				
Year	U.S. Primary Evidence	U.S. Contributory Evidence*	US Total	International All DNA Evidence*
2017	11	5	16	2
2016	17	2	19	5
2015	12	6	18	1
2014	9	12	21	2
2013	11	3	14	1
2012	19	2	21	2
2011	22	4	26	3
2010	18	4	21	1
2009	22	5	27	5
2008	18	3	20	4
2007	19	0	19	0
2006	19	2	21	0
2005	17	4	21	1
2004	13	1	14	5
2003	21	3	24	1
2002	23	0	23	1
2001	20	0	20	2
2000	15	1	16	2
1999	13	0	13	1
1998	4	0	4	3
1997	8	1	9	1
1996	14	3	17	0
1995	7	1	8	1
1994	8	3	11	0
1993	4	1	5	0
1992	5	1	6	1
1991	3	0	3	0
1990	1	0	1	0
1989	1	0	1	0
Total	374	68	442	45

* All international cases involved DNA as primary evidence.
** Contributory DNA evidence was insufficient to be relied on to exonerate the person, however, when combined with other exculpatory evidence it contributed to the person's exoneration.

Chart 4

Exonerations Relying On DNA Evidence in the U.S. and Internationally - 1989-2017

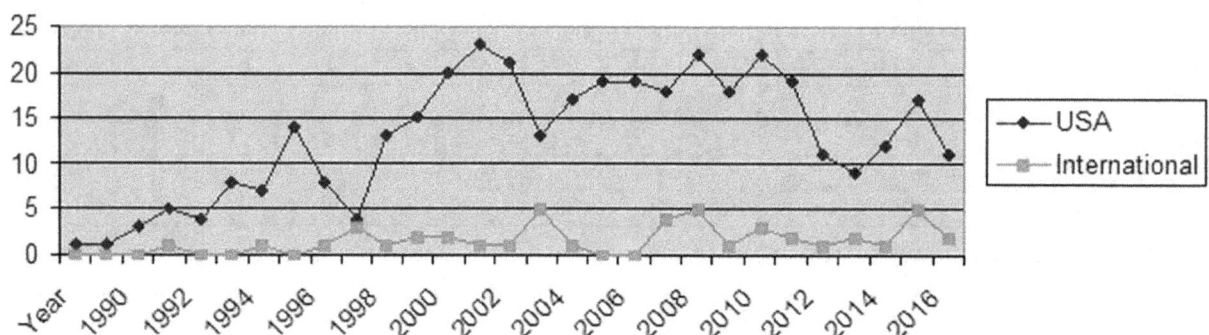

Chart 5
Pct. of U.S. Exonerations based on DNA evidence - 1989-2017

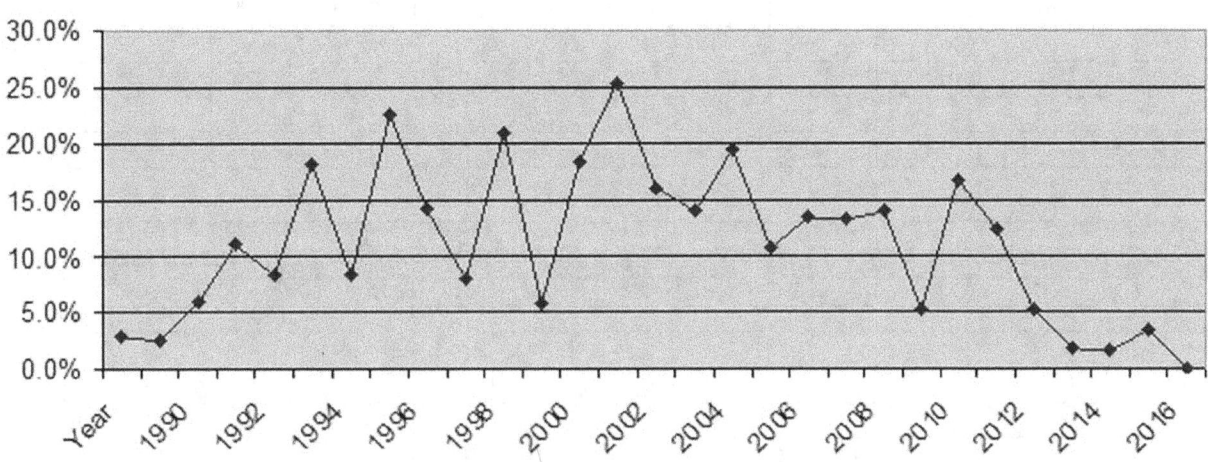

Table 15 — Number of Exonerations That Involved Conviction Integrity Unit (U.S.)											
Jurisdiction	2017	2016	2015	2014	2013	2012	2011	2010	2009	2008	Total
Harris County, TX	11	79	48	213	0	0	0	2	1	0	354
Cook County, IL	27	8	3	3	4	2	0	0	0	0	47
Cuyahoga County, OH	38	7	0	0	0	0	0	0	0	0	45
Dallas County, TX	3	0	0	3	0	6	4	3	4	7	30
Kings County, NY	3	4	7	10	0	0	0	0	0	0	24
Bexar County, TX	0	7	2	0	0	0	0	0	0	0	9
Multnomah County, OR	0	5	0	0	0	0	0	0	0	0	5
New York County, NY	0	0	0	0	1	3	0	0	0	0	4
Baltimore, MD	0	1	0	3	0	0	0	0	0	0	4
Tarrant County, TX	0	4	0	0	0	0	0	0	0	0	4
Lake County, Illinois	1	0	2	0	0	0	0	0	0	0	3
Philadelphia County, PA	1	2	0	0	0	0	0	0	0	0	3
Ventura County, CA	2	0	1	0	0	0	0	0	0	0	3
Los Angeles County, CA	2	1	0	0	0	0	0	0	0	0	3
Bronx County, NY	1	1	0	0	0	0	0	0	0	0	2
Santa Clara County, CA	0	0	0	0	0	1	0	0	0	0	1
Orleans Parish, LA	0	0	1	0	0	0	0	0	0	0	1
Clark County, NV	1	0	0	0	0	0	0	0	0	0	1
Suffolk County, MA	1	0	0	0	0	0	0	0	0	0	1
Total	91	119	64	232	5	12	4	5	5	7	544

Table 16 — Number of Exonerations Due To Original Investigation By Conviction Integrity Unit (U.S.)											
Years	2017	2016	2015	2014	2013	2012	2011	2010	2009	2008	Total
Cuyahoga County, OH	36	7	0	0	0	0	0	0	0	0	43
Kings County, NY	2	3	7	10	0	0	0	0	0	0	22
Harris County, TX	0	0	0	0	0	0	0	2	0	0	2
Dallas County, TX	0	0	0	0	0	0	0	0	0	1	1
Philadelphia County, PA	1	0	0	0	0	0	0	0	0	0	1
Ventura County, CA	1	0	0	0	0	0	0	0	0	0	1
Bronx County, NY	1	0	0	0	0	0	0	0	0	0	1
Los Angeles County, CA	1	0	0	0	0	0	0	0	0	0	1
Total	42	10	7	10	0	0	0	2	0	1	72

Table 17 — Number of Exonerated People By Years In Custody (U.S.)														
Years	2017	2016	2015	2014	2013	2012	2011	2010	2009	2008	10 yr total	1989-2017	Pre-1989	Total
1 to 9 yrs	61	65	91	46	52	57	47	70	44	56	589	1282	458	1740
10 to 19 yrs	19	23	25	36	32	31	28	29	36	23	282	603	70	673
20 to 29 yrs	33	35	27	15	16	12	18	11	19	18	204	278	21	299
30 to 39 yrs	6	1	6	9	3	2	0	3	2	1	33	38	5	43
40 and greater	1	0	0	0	0	0	0	0	0	0	0	2	0	2

Table 18 — Average Years Exonerated Person Was In Custody Before Release (All types of cases)														
Years	2017	2016	2015	2014	2013	2012	2011	2010	2009	2008	10 yr total	1989-2017	Pre-1989	Total Avg.
United States														
Men	11.7	8.6	7.6	10.3	10.5	10.3	10.6	8.7	12.4	9.8	9.8	9.4	5.0	8.3
Women	6.0	4.8	3.9	4.2	3.0	4.6	5.3	5.7	5.0	4.7	4.6	5.1	3.0	4.5
Combined	11.2	8.1	7.2	9.4	9.9	9.6	10.3	8.5	11.6	9.4	9.3	9.0	4.8	7.9
International														
Men	3.5	6.4	5.6	3.6	4.0	6.7	3.3	5.2	4.2	3.0	4.5	4.9	5.5	5.0
Women	2.4	5.5	2.5	0.9	1.3	3.9	3.6	1.8	0.9	1.2	2.4	3.1	2.6	3.1
Combined	3.3	6.3	5.1	3.3	3.9	6.5	2.8	4.6	3.9	2.8	4.2	4.7	3.5	4.6

Table 19 — Average Years Exonerated Person Was In Custody For Crime Of Violence (Violent crimes only)														
Years	2017	2016	2015	2014	2013	2012	2011	2010	2009	2008	10 yr total	1989-2017	Pre-1989	Total Avg.
United States														
Men	15.6	13.1	11.7	15.3	12.7	12.2	13.1	10.9	13.2	12.1	13.0	11.1	5.6	9.9
Women	7.0	11.2	8.0	6.9	4.4	6.8	7.6	6.7	5.8	5.9	7.1	6.3	3.9	6.0
Combined	14.7	13.0	11.4	14.3	12.2	11.7	12.8	10.7	12.4	11.6	12.5	10.7	5.5	9.6
International														
Men	3.8	7.6	6.5	4.1	6.6	7.7	5.3	6.0	5.5	3.2	5.5	5.8	6.9	5.9
Women	3.0	6.1	3.3	1.1	1.8	5.9	5.8	2.3	1.4	1.2	3.2	3.9	3.8	3.9
Combined	3.7	7.4	6.0	3.8	6.1	7.6	5.4	5.5	5.2	3.1	5.3	5.6	5.6	5.5

Chart 6

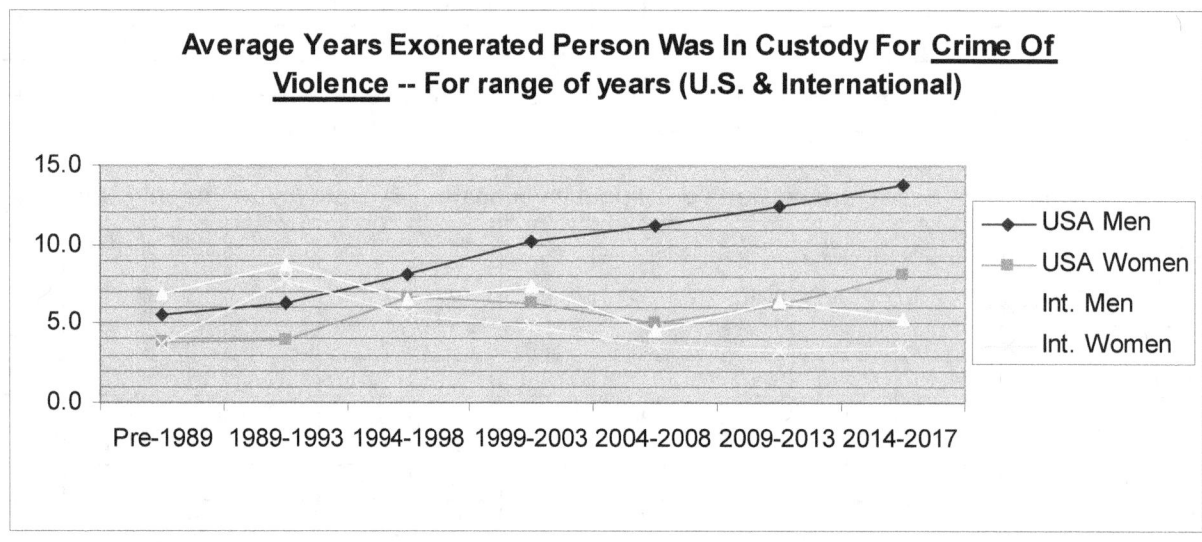

Average Years Exonerated Person Was In Custody For Crime Of Violence -- For range of years (U.S. & International)

Table 20 — Average Years Exonerated Person Was In Custody Before Release (NON-violent crimes only)

Years	2017	2016	2015	2014	2013	2012	2011	2010	2009	2008	10 yr total	1989-2017	Pre-1989	Total Avg.
United States														
Men	2.4	1.3	1.1	2.1	1.2	2.0	3.2	3.2	4.1	1.7	1.9	2.1	1.6	2.0
Women	0.4	0.1	0.7	1.2	0.8	1.7	1.8	0.5	0.8	0.0	0.8	1.6	1.0	1.5
Combined	2.3	1.1	1.1	1.9	1.1	1.9	3.1	3.1	3.4	1.6	1.8	2.0	1.4	1.9
International														
Men	1.6	1.6	2.0	1.0	2.8	1.3	0.7	2.3	1.2	1.6	1.9	2.1	1.6	2.0
Women	0.2	0.0	0.9	0.3	0.2	1.3	0.0	1.3	0.6	1.2	0.8	1.1	0.9	1.0
Combined	1.3	1.5	1.7	0.9	2.8	1.3	0.5	2.0	1.1	1.5	1.7	1.7	1.4	1.7

Chart 7

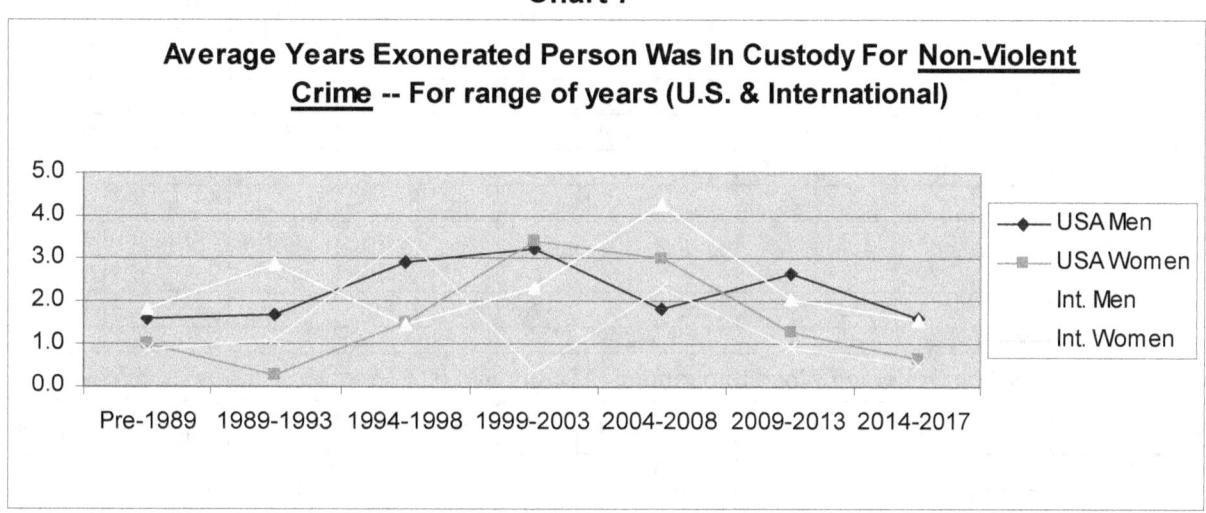

Average Years Exonerated Person Was In Custody For <u>Non-Violent Crime</u> -- For range of years (U.S. & International)

Table 21 — Average Years Exonerated Person Was In Custody Before Release (Homicide or Sexual Assault only)

Years	2017	2016	2015	2014	2013	2012	2011	2010	2009	2008	10 yr total	1989-2017	Pre-1989	Total Avg.
United States														
Men	16.5	15.3	14.5	16.9	15.1	13.6	14.6	12.2	14.3	13.5	14.7	12.4	6.2	11.0
Women	8.9	11.2	12.3	11.5	5.3	8.6	7.6	9.8	7.0	9.0	9.3	7.5	3.7	7.0
Combined	15.8	14.9	14.3	16.5	14.4	13.2	14.2	12.0	13.6	13.3	14.3	12.0	6.1	10.8
International														
Men	5.6	8.8	7.3	4.4	8.1	7.4	5.6	8.0	6.8	3.5	6.4	6.8	8.0	6.9
Women	3.6	7.9	4.1	0	2.1	5.6	5.8	2.4	2.1	1.5	4.1	4.8	2.8	4.8
Combined	5.3	8.8	6.8	4.4	7.4	7.3	5.6	7.1	6.6	3.3	6.2	6.6	7.6	6.7

Table 22 — Average Years Exonerated Person Was In Custody (NON-Homicide or Sexual Assault crimes of violence only)

Years	2017	2016	2015	2014	2013	2012	2011	2010	2009	2008	10 yr total	1989-2017	Pre-1989	Total Avg.
United States														
Men	9.7	2.5	3.5	5.5	3.3	6.1	7.4	6.3	5.8	6.5	5.3	4.9	3.0	4.4
Women	1.9	0	1.6	1.2	0	1.5	0	2.1	1.1	3.6	1.8	1.7	4.4	2.0
Combined	8.0	2.5	3.3	4.1	3.1	5.6	7.4	5.9	5.1	5.9	4.9	4.6	3.1	4.2
International														
Men	2.0	0.6	2.4	2.4	2.1	7.9	4.6	1.9	3.1	2.7	1.9	1.9	1.8	1.9
Women	1.2	2.3	0.6	1.1	0.3	7.0	0	1.5	0.7	0	0.8	1.1	0.9	1.0
Combined	2.0	1.0	2.0	1.9	2.0	7.9	4.6	1.9	2.9	2.6	1.7	1.7	1.4	1.7

Table 23 — Average Age Exonerated Person Was Taken Into Custody For Crime Of Violence (U.S. & Int.)														
Years	2017	2016	2015	2014	2013	2012	2011	2010	2009	2008	10 yr total	1989-2017	Pre-1989	Total Avg.
United States														
Men	46.9	43.7	41.0	43.0	41.1	40.4	42.0	40.6	40.6	42.0	42.1	40.3	34.1	39.9
Women	34.3	43.2	47.1	35.1	31.0	42.0	42.0	36.8	43.0	44.4	40.1	38.7	36.3	38.6
Combined	45.5	43.6	41.5	42.0	40.6	40.6	42.0	40.4	40.8	42.2	41.9	40.2	34.2	39.8
International														
Men	42.4	37.7	39.1	40.1	42.6	40.5	37.2	43.6	36.8	35.9	39.5	39.9	34.5	39.7
Women	43.2	41.5	31.4	44.8	42.0	51.5	38.0	29.8	24.0.	26.0	37.2	36.5	30.7	36.2
Combined	42.6	38.3	37.5	40.5	42.6	41.3	37.3	41.2	36.1	34.9	39.2	39.5	34.1	39.3

Table 24 — Average Age Exonerated Person Was Taken Into Custody For Non-Violent Crime (U.S. & Int.)														
Years	2017	2016	2015	2014	2013	2012	2011	2010	2009	2008	10 yr total	1989-2017	Pre-1989	Total Avg.
United States														
Men	39.5	37.7	34.9	38.3	40.0	39.3	44.5	38.5	50.3	33.1	38.1	39.3	39.9	39.3
Women	39.0	36.0	36.2	34.5	32.5	36.0	60.0	43.0	39.0	0.0	36.3	37.0	23.0	36.6
Combined	39.4	37.5	35.2	37.5	38.3	38.6	45.5	38.7	48.3	33.1	37.8	38.9	37.9	38.9
International														
Men	36.9	35.7	35.8	37.6	48.8	32.3	38.9	43.9	43.7	41.3	40.1	41.2	33.0	40.1
Women	40.0	42.0	39.0	28.4	31.0	0.0	39.3	37.0	37.7	53.5	34.3	34.2	24.0	33.5
Combined	37.3	37.3	37.1	33.9	43.5	32.3	39.	41.8	41.7	44.4	40.1	39.2	31.5	38.3

Table 25 — Average Age Of Person When Exonerated (ALL crimes) (U.S. & Int.)														
Years	2017	2016	2015	2014	2013	2012	2011	2010	2009	2008	10 yr total	1989-2017	Pre-1989	Total Avg.
United States														
Men	45.3	41.8	38.9	41.3	40.9	40.1	42.4	40.2	41.6	40.1	41.1	40.1	34.7	39.8
Women	34.7	40.3	40.8	34.8	31.8	39.4	46.5	38.0	42.2	44.4	38.6	38.1	33.6	37.9
Combined	44.3	41.7	39.1	40.3	40.2	40.0	42.6	40.1	41.6	40.3	40.9	39.9	34.7	39.6
International														
Men	40.8	37.4	38.7	39.0	44.6	39.9	38.1	43.7	37.9	36.8	39.6	40.1	33.8	39.8
Women	42.7	41.6	33.3	31.4	35.4	51.5	39.0	32.5	32.2	35.2	35.7	35.6	26.9	35.1
Combined	41.3	38.1	37.4	37.0	42.9	40.7	38.2	41.4	37.3	36.5	38.9	39.4	32.8	39.0

Chart 8
Average Age Of Person When Exonerated Of Violent Or Non-Violent Crime -- For range of years (U.S. & International)

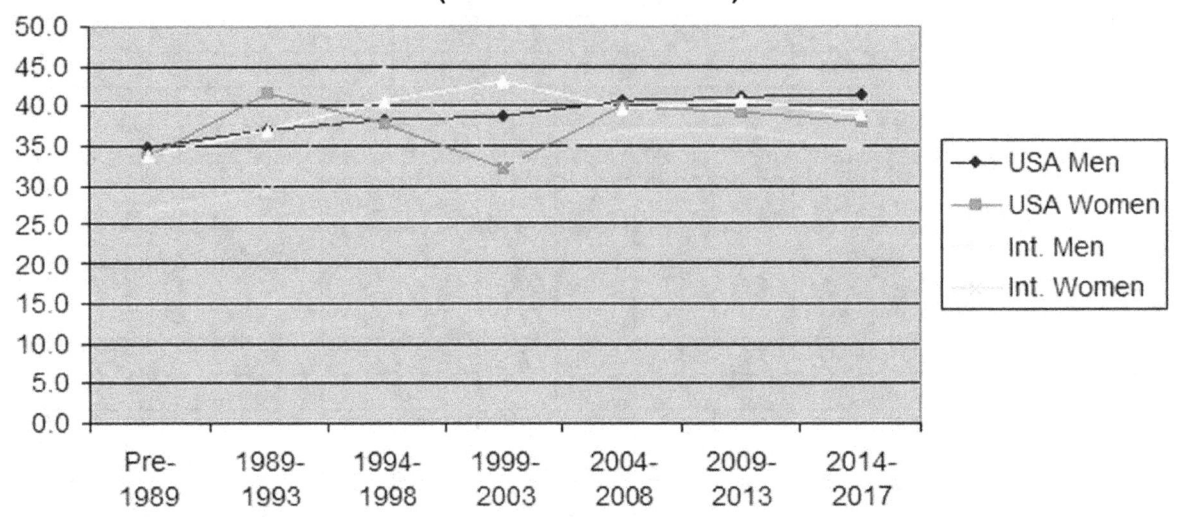

Table 26 — Number of Exonerated People By County (14 or more) (U.S.)															
County/Parish/Borough	State	Major City	2017	2016	2015	2014	2013	2012	2011	2010	2009	2008	10 yr total	1989-2017	Pre-1989	Total
Suffolk	MA	Boston	15,571	1	0	1	1	0	0	0	0	2	15,576	15,598	26	15,624
Middlesex	MA	Lowell	2,169	2	1	0	1	0	0	0	0	1	2,174	2,182	7	2,189
Essex	MA	Salem	1,067	0	1	0	0	0	0	2	0	0	1,070	1,077	27	1,104
Norfolk	MA	Quincy	965	0	0	0	1	1	1	0	0	0	968	969	3	972
Philadelphia	PA	Philadelphia	2	147	397	110	53	0	2	1	0	0	712	773	10	783777
Bristol	MA	New Bedford	777	1	0	0	0	0	1	0	0	0	779	782	0	782
Plymouth	MA	Middleborough	703	0	1	0	0	1	0	3	0	0	708	708	2	710
Harris	TX	Houston	19	80	53	214	3	4	1	4	3	1	382	398	3	401
Los Angeles	CA	Los Angeles	4	2	4	3	4	8	6	2	7	4	44	256	48	304
Barnstable	MA	Barnstable	303	0	0	0	0	0	0	0	0	0	303	303	0	303
Cook	IL	Chicago	37	13	6	14	13	10	11	4	7	6	121	200	25	225
Camden	NJ	Camden	0	0	1	0	0	0	0	0	172	0	0	173	174	177
New York	NY	New York City	2	3	11	5	5	7	5	0	3	6	47	70	57	127
Kings	NY	New York City	3	7	15	15	5	2	1	3	1	1	53	92	27	119
Wayne	MI	Detroit	7	4	0	5	4	1	0	6	3	3	33	53	32	85
Cuyahoga	OH	Cleveland	39	10	1	5	0	1	5	3	1	1	66	73	5	78
Bronx	NY	New York City	1	2	0	4	6	2	3	3	1	0	22	48	14	62
Queens	NY	New York City	1	2	3	1	1	2	4	2	1	0	17	37	13	50
Tulsa	OK	Tulsa	0	2	0	2	0	1	7	17	2	0	31	39	0	39
Swisher	TX	Tulia	0	0	1	0	0	0	2	0	0	0	3	38	0	38
District of Columbia	DC	District of Columbia	1	1	2	3	1	5	1	0	3	0	17	25	11	36
Suffolk	NY	Southhampton	2	2	2	0	1	7	1	0	1	2	18	24	11	35
Orleans	LA	New Orleans	5	2	1	1	1	2	1	0	0	0	13	29	2	31
Baltimore	MD	Baltimore	6	2	0	3	0	1	1	1	0	1	15	22	7	29
King	WA	Seattle	0	1	1	0	1	0	0	1	2	0	6	21	7	28
Charleston	SC	Charleston	0	1	0	0	0	0	0	0	0	0	0	1	24	25
Kern	CA	Bakersfield	0	0	0	0	0	0	1	0	0	1	2	25	0	25
Milwaukee	WI	Milwaukee	0	1	2	0	0	0	0	2	6	0	11	24	0	24
San Diego	CA	San Diego	1	0	0	3	1	1	3	0	1	1	11	23	1	24
Miami-Dade	FL	Miami	1	1	2	0	0	0	0	1	0	0	5	14	10	24
Dukes	MA	Edgartown	24	0	0	0	0	0	0	0	0	0	24	24	0	24
Monroe	NY	Rochester	0	2	2	1	0	1	0	2	0	0	8	12	11	23
Richmond	VA	Richmond	0	7	8	0	0	1	0	2	0	0	18	22	1	23
Broward	FL	Fort Lauderdale	0	1	3	0	0	1	0	1	1	0	7	17	5	22
Erie	NY	Buffalo	1	1	2	1	1	0	0	2	1	1	10	14	8	22
Montgomery	TX	Conroe	2	7	5	1	0	2	0	2	0	0	19	22	0	22
East Baton Rouge	LA	Baton Rouge	0	0	0	0	0	0	0	0	0	0	0	1	18	19
Clark	NV	Las Vegas	3	3	0	1	0	0	1	0	1	0	9	16	3	19
Oklahoma	OK	Oklahoma City	0	2	1	0	1	0	1	0	2	0	7	13	6	19
Richland	OH	Mansfield	0	0	1	1	0	0	0	0	0	14	16	18	0	18
Oakland	MI	Oak Park	0	0	0	3	2	1	0	4	1	1	12	14	4	18
Berrien	MI	Benton Harbor	1	0	0	0	0	0	0	1	14	0	16	18	0	18
Allegheny	PA	Pittsburgh	0	1	0	0	0	1	1	0	0	0	3	14	3	17
Santa Clara	CA	Cupertino	0	0	1	0	0	1	0	1	1	1	5	16	0	16
Maricopa	AZ	Phoenix	0	1	1	0	0	2	0	2	0	1	7	15	1	16
Jefferson	AL	Birmingham	0	0	2	0	0	1	2	0	0	0	5	16	0	16
San Francisco	CA	San Francisco	0	0	2	0	0	0	1	2	0	0	5	8	8	16
Franklin	OH	Columbus	0	0	0	0	0	0	0	0	1	1	2	9	7	16
York	NC	Rock Hill	0	0	14	0	0	0	0	0	0	0	14	14	0	14
Bexar	TX	San Antonio	0	8	3	0	0	1	1	0	0	0	13	13	1	14
Orange	CA	Santa Ana	0	1	0	2	0	1	0	2	0	1	7	14	0	14
Hillsborough	FL	Tampa	0	0	1	0	1	0	0	0	0	1	3	12	2	14
Hampden	MA	Springfield	1	0	0	0	2	3	1	1	0	0	8	11	3	14
Travis	TX	Austin	2	0	1	1	0	1	0	0	2	0	7	14	0	14
Nantucket	MA	Nantucket	14	0	0	0	0	0	0	0	0	0	14	14	0	14

Table 27 — Number of Exonerated People By Country – International Cases Only														
Country	2017	2016	2015	2014	2013	2012	2011	2010	2009	2008	10 yr total	1989-2016	Pre-1989	Total
Afghanistan	0	0	0	0	0	0	0	1	0	0	1	1	0	1
Angola	0	0	0	0	0	0	18	0	0	0	18	18	0	18
Australia	10	14	10	11	16	8	13	6	11	22	121	166	16	182
Austria	1	0	0	0	0	0	0	0	0	0	1	1	0	1
Bahamas	1	1	5	0	2	0	1	0	0	0	10	10	0	10
Bahrain	0	0	0	0	0	9	0	0	0	1	10	12	0	12
Bangladesh	0	0	3	0	0	0	0	0	1	0	4	4	0	4
Barbados	2	2	0	0	0	0	0	0	0	0	4	4	1	5
Belarus	0	0	0	0	0	0	0	3	0	0	3	3	0	3
Belgium	0	0	0	0	0	0	0	0	0	7	7	7	0	7
Belize	1	0	2	0	0	0	0	1	4	0	8	10	0	10
Bermuda	0	1	2	0	2	0	0	0	0	0	5	6	0	6
Bhutan	0	2	0	0	0	0	0	0	0	0	2	2	0	2
Botswana	0	0	0	0	0	0	0	0	0	2	2	2	0	2
Brazil	0	0	1	0	0	0	0	0	0	0	1	1	0	1
Brunei Darussalam	0	0	0	0	0	0	0	0	0	1	1	1	0	1
Bulgaria	0	0	0	0	0	0	0	0	1	0	1	1	0	1
Cambodia	0	0	0	0	1	0	0	0	0	0	1	1	0	1
Canada	7	7	8	4	2	5	4	7	6	9	59	106	6	112
Cayman Islands	0	0	0	0	1	0	3	1	1	0	6	6	0	6
Chile	0	0	0	0	0	0	0	0	0	0	0	3	0	3
China	4	15	6	2	2	2	0	3	0	0	34	40	1	41
Colombia	0	0	1	0	1	0	0	0	0	1	3	3	0	3
Costa Rica	0	0	6	0	1	0	0	0	0	0	7	8	0	8
Croatia	0	1	0	0	0	2	0	0	0	0	3	7	0	7
Cuba	0	0	0	0	0	0	0	1	0	0	1	1	0	1
Cyprus	0	0	0	0	0	0	0	0	0	0	3	3	0	3
Czech Republic	0	0	0	0	0	0	4	0	0	0	4	4	0	4
Denmark	0	0	0	0	0	0	0	0	0	0	0	1	0	1
Egypt	1	7	12	0	0	0	0	2	1	0	23	24	0	24
Fiji	2	0	1	0	4	2	5	0	0	5	19	19	0	19
Finland	0	4	2	0	0	0	1	0	0	0	7	7	0	7
France	0	0	1	3	0	2	1	0	6	0	13	20	6	26
Gambia	1	0	0	0	0	0	0	0	0	0	1	1	0	1
Germany	50,000	0	0	0	0	2	0	0	1	0	50,003	50,016	27	50,043
Ghana	1	1	4	0	0	0	1	0	2	0	9	12	0	12
Greece	0	1	0	0	0	0	12	0	0	0	13	15	0	15
Guatemala	0	0	0	0	0	0	0	0	0	0	0	0	3	3
Hong Kong	3	5	2	6	6	2	7	1	2	0	34	39	0	39
Hungary	0	0	0	0	0	0	1	0	0	0	1	3	0	3
India	83	32	40	19	18	52	7	4	5	3	263	272	6	278
Indonesia	0	0	0	0	0	0	0	0	1	3	4	7	0	7
Iran	0	0	0	3	0	0	0	0	0	1	4	4	0	4
Ireland	3	2	5	3	0	0	0	1	1	1	16	29	3	32
Isle of Man	0	0	0	1	0	0	0	0	0	0	1	1	0	1
Israel	0	1	1	16	0	0	0	1	1	0	20	28	1	29
Italy	1	3	8	16	0	3	1	2	1	0	35	38	1	39
Jamaica	2	0	0	0	0	3	1	0	7	3	16	21	5	26
Japan	0	3	2	1	0	1	2	2	0	1	13	16	10	26
Jersey	0	0	0	0	0	0	0	1	0	0	1	1	0	1
Kenya	1	0	1	6	1	3	4	0	4	2	22	29	0	29
Kosovo	0	0	0	0	0	0	0	0	1	0	1	1	0	1
Kuwait	0	1	0	0	0	0	0	0	0	0	1	2	0	2
Latvia	0	0	0	0	0	0	0	0	0	0	1	1	0	1
Libya	0	0	0	0	2	0	0	0	0	0	8	8	0	8
Lithuania	0	0	0	0	1	0	0	0	0	0	1	1	0	1
Malawi	0	19	0	0	0	0	0	0	0	0	21	22	0	22
Malaysia	3	4	2	7	2	0	0	2	3	7	30	37	0	37
Maldives	0	0	0	0	2	0	0	0	0	0	2	2		2
Malta	1	7	0	0	0	0	0	0	0	0	8	8	0	8

Country	2017	2016	2015	2014	2013	2012	2011	2010	2009	2008	10 yr total	1989-2016	Pre-1989	Total
Mauritius	0	1	0	0	0	0	0	0	0	0	1	1	0	1
Mexico	0	0	1	0	1	1	0	0	0	0	3	9	0	9
Mongolia	0	0	3	0	0	0	0	0	0	0	3	3	0	3
Morocco	0	0	0	1	0	0	0	0	0	1	2	2	0	2
Namibia	1	1	0	2	1	1	0	0	0	0	6	7	0	7
Nauru	0	0	0	0	0	0	0	0	0	0	0	0	1	1
Netherlands	0	0	0	0	0	0	0	2	1	0	3	6	1	7
Netherlands (Dutch)	0	0	0	0	2	0	0	0	0	0	2	2	0	2
New Caledonia	0	0	0	0	0	0	0	0	1	0	1	1	0	1
New Zealand	2	7	13	11	4	0	2	4	4	11	58	74	2	76
Nicaragua	0	0	0	0	0	0	0	0	0	0	1	1	0	1
Nigeria	3	0	3	0	3	1	2	0	0	0	12	19	1	20
North Korea	0	0	0	0	0	0	0	0	2	0	2	2	0	2
Northern Mariana Islands	0	0	1	1	1	0	0	0	0	0	3	3	0	3
Norway	0	0	0	0	0	0	0	0	11	13	42	70	0	70
Pakistan	7	2	9	0	0	2	0	0	1	0	21	30	0	30
Peru	0	2	0	0	0	1	0	1	0	0	4	4	0	4
Philippines	0	1	1	0	0	0	0	7	1	0	10	10	1	11
Poland	0	0	0	0	0	0	0	0	0	0	0	1	0	1
Portugal	0	1	0	0	0	0	0	0	0	0	1	1	0	1
Qatar	0	0	0	2	0	0	0	0	0	0	2	2	0	2
Russian Federation	2	0	0	0	1	0	0	0	0	0	3	4	15	19
Rwanda	0	0	0	0	0	0	0	0	0	1	1	1	0	1
Saint Kitts and Nevis	0	0	1	0	1	0	0	1	4	4	12	12	0	12
Saint Lucia	0	0	0	0	0	0	0	0	0	0	1	1	0	1
Samoa	1	0	0	0	0	0	0	0	0	0	1	1	0	1
Saudi Arabia	0	0	0	0	0	0	0	0	0	0	0	7	0	7
Senegal	0	0	0	0	0	0	0	0	9	0	9	9	0	9
Serbia	0	0	1	0	1	0	0	2	1	0	5	5	0	5
Seychelles	0	0	0	0	0	0	0	0	0	0	0	0	1	1
Sierra Leone	0	0	0	0	1	0	1	0	0	0	2	2	0	2
Singapore	1	0	0	1	2	3	0	0	1	2	10	11	1	12
Somalia	0	0	0	0	2	0	0	0	0	0	2	2	0	2
South Africa	8	1	3	2	0	1	0	0	0	6	21	38	2	40
South Korea	0	4	0	0	1	0	0	0	0	3	16	17	0	17
Spain	0	0	0	1	0	0	5	0	0	4	10	16	0	16
Sri Lanka	0	0	0	0	0	0	0	0	0	1	1	1	1	2
Sudan	0	0	1	1	0	0	0	0	0	0	6	6	0	6
Swaziland	0	0	0	0	1	0	0	0	0	0	1	1	0	1
Sweden	1	5	0	1	2	4	1	1	0	2	17	21	0	21
Switzerland	0	1	0	0	0	0	0	1	2	0	4	5	0	5
Taiwan	0	1	0	0	0	0	2	0	0	0	3	3	0	3
Tanzania	0	1	2	13	1	1	0	0	1	1	20	33	0	33
Thailand	1	0	0	0	0	0	0	0	0	0	1	7	0	7
Tonga	0	0	0	0	0	1	0	1	1	0	3	3	0	3
Trinidad and Tobago	0	0	0	1	1	0	0	1	5	0	9	10	0	10
Tunisia	0	0	0	0	1	0	0	0	0	0	1	1	0	1
Turkey	1	275	2	1	63	0	0	0	0	0	342	345	0	345
Turks and Caicos Islands	0	0	0	0	0	5	0	0	0	0	5	5	0	5
Uganda	0	1	0	1	0	1	0	1	0	0	4	8	0	8
Ukraine	0	0	0	0	0	0	0	0	0	0	0	1	0	1
United Arab Emirates	1	1	0	0	7	1	5	0	3	0	18	19	0	19
United Kingdom (Great Britain)	49,046	57	75	96	57	30	53	32	46	42	49,534	50,035	107	50,142
U.N. Court in the Hague	0	1	0	0	0	0	0	0	0	1	2	2	0	2
Vanuatu	12	6	0	0	4	0	1	0	0	0	23	37	1	38
Vietnam	0	0	1	1	1	0	0	0	0	1	4	20	1	21
Virgin Islands (British)	0	0	0	2	0	0	1	0	0	0	4	4	0	4
Zambia	0	0	0	0	2	4	0	1	0	0	7	7	0	7
Zimbabwe	4	3	1	4	0	0	1	4	1	1	19	22	0	22
Total	99,219	505	243	240	225	143	160	97	156	163	101,161	102,086	221	102,307

Table 28 — Number of Exonerated People By Type of Crime (International)														
Type	2017	2016	2015	2014	2013	2012	2011	2010	2009	2008	10 yr total	1989-2017	Pre-1989	Total
Homicide	44	44	62	51	28	38	25	19	32	41	384	669	52	721
Homicide/Sex	1	5	1	3	3	1	2	7	0	1	24	33	1	34
Sexual Assault/Rape/Indecent Assault	10	9	8	11	9	7	11	13	18	19	115	231	4	235
Child Sex Assault/Abuse	9	7	10	9	4	0	5	6	3	4	57	86	1	87
Robbery/Theft/Burglary/Extortion	4	8	12	9	10	7	8	5	8	10	81	173	46	219
Assault	2	20	13	8	6	3	4	6	24	25	111	153	13	166
Drug	6	2	12	4	8	2	4	7	9	10	64	112	4	116
Fraud/Forgery/Embezzlement/Bribery	16	25	23	4	12	2	11	9	10	7	119	160	7	167
Child Abuse/Assault	0	0	0	2	0	0	0	0	0	0	2	6	0	6
Violent Other	58	291	10	17	15	47	7	8	17	30	500	579	45	624
Non-violent Other	99,069	94	92	122	130	46	83	17	35	16	99,704	99,884	48	99,932
Total	99,219	505	243	240	225	153	160	97	156	163	101,161	102,086	221	102,307

Table 29 — Number of Exonerated People By Method of Exoneration (International)														
Type	2017	2016	2015	2014	2013	2012	2011	2010	2009	2008	10 yr total	1989-2017	Pre-1989	Total
Acquitted by reviewing Court	167	428	130	81	125	102	65	36	30	22	1186	1299	15	1314
Acquitted after retrial	5	13	13	4	7	0	8	6	4	11	71	119	16	135
Conviction quashed	42	51	68	98	38	18	14	20	31	15	395	605	14	619
Charges dismissed	5	11	22	56	54	31	67	35	86	114	481	966	112	1078
Pardoned	49,000	0	8	0	1	0	5	0	1	1	49,016	49,096	13	49,109
Legislative	50,000	0	0	0	0	0	0	0	0	1	50,001	50,001	17	50,018

Table 30 — Number of Exonerated Persons Involved In A Case With A Co-Defendant (International)														
Type	2017	2016	2015	2014	2013	2012	2011	2010	2009	2008	10 yr total	1989-2017	Pre-1989	Total
2 Co-defendants	25	15	20	28	30	20	5	7	9	18	177	264	15	279
3 Co-defendants	0	12	24	12	3	15	9	11	13	9	108	168	30	198
4 Co-defendants	8	16	4	0	8		12	0	4	16	68	110	1	111
5 Co-defendants	10	10	5	10	0	10	15	0	5	10	75	85	5	90
6 Co-defendants	6	6	6	12	0	0	5	1	0	0	36	60	0	60
7 Co-defendants	0	0	0	14	0	0	0	7	0	7	28	42	6	48
8 Co-defendants	9	8	7	0	0	0	0	0	8	0	32	40	0	40
9 Co-defendants	0	0	0	0	0	9	0	0	9	0	18	0	0	18
10 Co-defendants	0	0	0	0	0	0	0	0	0	0	0	9	0	9
11 Co-defendants	0	0	0	0	0	22	0	0	0	0	22	0	0	22
12 Co-defendants	12	0	12	0	0	0	12	0	0	0	36	36	0	36
13 Co-defendants	0	0	0	0	0	0	0	0	0	0	0	0	13	13
16 Co-defendants	0	0	0	16	0	0	0	0	0	0	16	16	0	16
17 Co-defendants	0	0	0	0	0	17	0	0	0	0	17	17	0	17
18 Co-defendants	0	0	0	0	0	0	18	0	0	0	18	18	0	18
19 Co-defendants	0	19	0	0	0	0	0	0	0	0	19	19	0	19
20 Co-defendants	0	0	0	0	0	0	20	0	0	0	20	20	0	20
29 Co-defendants	0	0	0	29	0	0	0	0	0	0	29	29	0	29
35 Co-defendants	35	0	0	0	0	0	0	0	0	0	35	35	0	35
Total	105	86	78	121	41	93	96	26	48	60	719	1,008	70	1,078

Map 2 — World Map Showing 120 Countries With A Known Exoneration (See Table 27's Total column for data.)

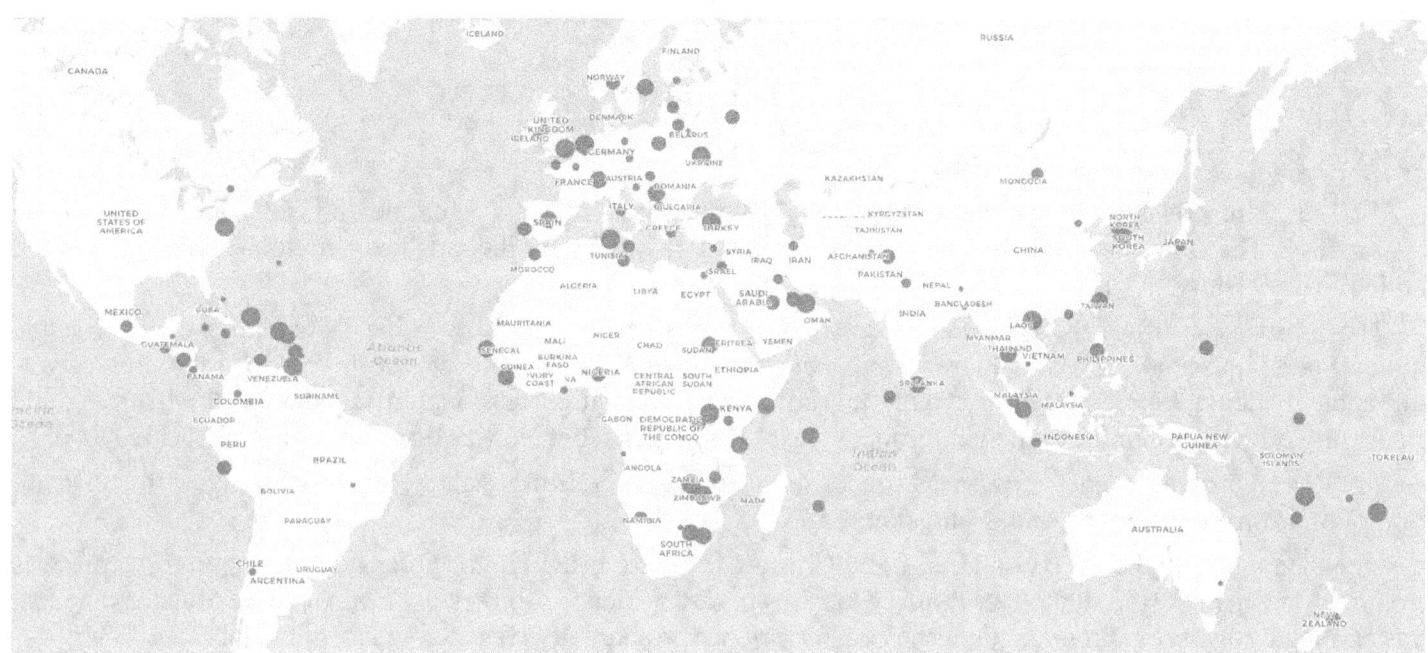

Map created with Carto.com.

21,587 People Exonerated In Massachusetts Due To Fraudulent Crime Lab Testing

By Hans Sherrer
Justice Denied
May 6, 2017

21,587 drug related convictions were vacated by the Massachusetts Supreme Judicial Court on April 19, 2017. The Court also ordered dismissal of the cases. It was by far the most exonerations on a single day in United States history.[19]

The prosecution of all the cases relied on a "drug certificate" signed by Annie Dookhan, a chemist at the Hinton State Laboratory. It is now known Dookhan's certification an illegal drug was involved in those cases was unreliable evidence: She engaged in extensive criminal activity and professional misconduct in the handling and processing of evidence in the crime lab for many years before her sabotage was discovered in June 2011.

The 21,587 cases were in nine Massachusetts counties: Suffolk; Middlesex; Essex; Norfolk; Bristol; Plymouth; Barnstable; Dukes; and, Nantucket.

Dookhan was 26 when she was hired in 2003 as a Chemist I at the Hinton forensic drug laboratory. She was promoted to Chemist II in 2005. Her primary job was to test evidence samples in criminal cases to determine if it was an illegal substance. From the time she began work her productivity was the highest in the lab.

After Dookhan had worked in the lab for eight years, an evidence officer discovered in June 2011 that she had not properly signed out 90 drug samples. Several days later three lab supervisors met to discuss that the evidence log book didn't show the drug samples had been signed out to her ... or anyone else. The next day Dookhan was confronted about the evidence log, and a new situation: In the hours since the three supervisors had met, the initials of an evidence officer had been inserted in the log book next to the drug samples. The evidence officer denied initialing the log book and Dookhan denied knowledge of the discrepancy.

The lab initiated an internal investigation. Dookhan admitted she had forged the evidence officer's initials and post-dated entries in the log book. She was suspended from performing lab work on new cases. However, she remained on the lab's payroll, and her superiors allowed her to testify in court about cases she was involved in up to the time of her suspension. Prosecutors and defendants in those cases were not informed Dookhan had been suspended from performing laboratory tests because of her dishonesty.

In February 2012 Dookhan ceased testifying in court when the district attorneys in the seven counties that used the services of the Hinton drug lab were notified Dookhan had been suspended eight months earlier. The DA's could no longer subpoena her as an expert witness because they would be legally obligated to provide a defendant's lawyer with the evidence of her dishonest conduct. She was placed on paid administrative leave, and resigned a month later in March 2012.

As a cost-cutting move, in July 2012 control of the Hinton drug lab was transferred from the Massachusetts Department of Public Health to the Office of Public Safety and Security. The Massachusetts State Police initiated an investigation into Dookhan's practices before she was suspended from performing lab work.

The State Police discovered during their interview of Dookhan on August 28, 2012, something she had not told her lab supervisors: she admitted "dry labbing" evidence samples. "Dry labbing" describes a technician visually identifying samples without performing a chemical test. Dookhan also admitted that when she had evidence samples from different cases that appeared similar, she would select a sample from a case for testing to verify it was the drug she believed it was. She then assumed all the untested samples were the same drug -- and reported on the "drug certificate" for those cases the sample had tested positive for that drug. She also admitted to fabricating evidence in drug cases by adding cocaine to samples that didn't have cocaine present.

Furthermore, Dookhan admitted to the State Police that she had been engaging in insubstantial lab practices

---

[19] "21,587 People Exonerated In Massachusetts Due To Fraudulent Crime Lab Testing," By Hans Sherrer, *Justice Denied*, May 6, 2017, online at: http://justicedenied.org/wordpress/archives/3635 .

for a number of years. That she had been doing so from around the time she began working at the lab was suggested by the fact that starting during her first year of employment, "She reported test results on samples at rates consistently much higher than any other chemist in the lab."[20]

The State Police discovered that Dookhan regularly reported testing over 500 samples per month. That was five times the typical workload of a laboratory drug chemist. Yet, Dookhan's supervisors and colleagues told the State Patrol they never saw her using a microscope, and she frequently misidentified samples. The disregard of the numerous red flags there was something amiss with Dookhan's work suggested a "See no evil, speak no evil" culture in the drug lab. All was OK as long as she generated results that made the lab look productive and assisted prosecutors secure convictions.

The discovery by State Police investigators that Dookhan took the shortcut of failing to conduct any test in innumerable cases in which she reported a positive drug test result, explained how she was able to be the most productive drug technician in the crime lab for eight years.

The State Police investigation also discovered that when she testified during at least 14 criminal trials, Dookhan burnished her expert credentials by lying that she had a Master's degree in Chemistry from the University of Massachusetts at Boston (UMass). She not only didn't have a Master's degree in Chemistry, but she not had never enrolled in any master's level classes at UMass. Dookhan's perjury about her education was relied on by judges to admit her as an expert witness, and it established the veracity of the drug certificate of her testing admitted into evidence. It was found that she also falsely stated in her resume that she had a UMass Master's degree in Chemistry. The Hinton lab didn't check Dookhan's educational qualifications when she was hired as a chemist in 2003.

Dookhan's dishonest embellishment of her qualifications and experience went beyond falsely claiming she had a Masters degree in Chemistry: She fabricated job titles for herself that included she had been a "special agent of operations" for the FBI and other federal agencies, and that she had been an "on-call terrorism supervisor."

The *Boston Globe* reported that Norfolk County prosecutors ignored multiple warnings that Dookhan was a chronic liar. Almost two years before she was suspended her husband, Surrendranath Dookhan, sent multiple text messages warning about her dishonesty. One of the text messages stated: "This is Annie's Husband do not believe her, she's a liar, she's always lying."[21] (Annie Sadiyya Khan adopted her husband's last name when they married in 2004.)

Disregarding the warnings by Dookhan's husband that she was a pathological liar was emblematic of the professional affection prosecutors had for her: They loved her because she was so reliable in providing "scientific" evidence to support a conviction. Prosecutors were so happy with her assistance that they congratulated her in emails and took her out for cocktails as a reward for her work. One district attorney called Dookhan a member of the prosecutor's "dream team."[22]

Dookhan even provided "fake" evidence to order.

The *Boston Globe* reported that in May 2010 Norfolk Assistant District Attorney George Papachristos "told her he needed a marijuana sample to weigh at least 50 pounds so that he could charge the owners with drug trafficking. "Any help would be greatly appreciated!" he wrote, punctuating each sentence with a long string of exclamation points. "Thank you!" Two hours later, Dookhan responded: "OK . . . definitely Trafficking, over 80 lbs." Papachristos thanked her profusely."[23] Papachristos resigned in October 2012 after his very friendly relationship with Dookhan was reported by the *Boston Globe*.

The Hinton lab's quality controls were so deficient at detecting fraud, that an audit of Dookhan's work in 2010 failed to find anything out of the ordinary, except that she was exceptionally efficient at processing case evidence.

Dookhan was arrested on September 28, 2012. She charged with two counts of obstruction of justice and one

---

[20] Source: https://scholar.google.com/scholar_case?case=13900209628902371114&q=471+Mass.+465,+30+N.E.3d+806&hl=en&as_sdt=6,48
[21] Source: http://www.necn.com/news/new-england/_NECN__Husband_of_Former_Mass__Chemist_Reportedly_Tried_to_Warn_Prosecutor_NECN-247711081.html
[22] Source: http://www.policestateusa.com/2013/annie-dookhan-crime-lab-chemist-falsified-evidence/
[23] Source: http://www.policestateusa.com/2013/annie-dookhan-crime-lab-chemist-falsified-evidence/

count of falsifying her academic records. She was released on $10,000 bail.

After her arrest Dookhan was indicted for crimes that included: evidence tampering, obstruction of justice, perjury, and falsely claiming to hold a graduate degree.

Dookhan agreed to plead guilty to 27 counts of tampering with evidence in exchange for the dropping of all other charges. She didn't state why she acted as she did, but some of her communications suggested she didn't like drug users and dealers and wanted them off the street. She was apparently oblivious to the harm her crusade was causing innocent people to suffer.

On November 22, 2013 she was sentenced to three to five years imprisonment and two years probation by Judge Carol S. Ball in Suffolk Superior Court. Ball said in sentencing Dookhan, "Innocent persons were incarcerated, guilty persons have been released to further endanger the public, millions and millions of public dollars are being expended to deal with the chaos Ms. Dookhan created, and the integrity of the criminal justice system has been shaken to the core."[24] Dookhan's bail was revoked and she was taken into custody to begin serving her sentence.

Dookhan was paroled in April 2016 after less than 2-1/2 years in prison.

As Judge Ball had alluded to, there was significant legal fallout from Dookhan's conduct.

More than 21,000 defendants had been convicted based on the prosecution's reliance on the evidence of a Dookhan "drug certificate."

A number of defendants filed a petition to withdraw their guilty plea when the prosecution's case was primarily based on the evidence of a Dookhan "drug certificate." They pled guilty under the pressure of Dookhan's purported incriminating evidence that made their acquittal after a trial nearly impossible. They asserted their guilty plea "was involuntarily induced by government misconduct that since has been discovered."[25]

In 2014 the Massachusetts Supreme Judicial Court (SJC) ruled that "where the defendant proffers a drug certificate from the defendant's case signed by Dookhan on the line labeled "Assistant Analyst," the defendant is entitled to a conclusive presumption that egregious government misconduct occurred in the defendant's case."[26]

The SJC had to then grapple with the issue of whether the tens of thousands of affected defendants would be dealt with on a case by case basis to determine if a defendant was prejudiced, or if the court would issue a global ruling affecting all of the defendants.

The district attorneys of the seven counties had mailed a written notice to defendants whose case Dookhan's had worked on. The notice explained they could explore with a lawyer the possibility of withdrawing their plea or moving for a new trial based on her misconduct.

The Dookhan court cases had effectively been consolidated by the SJC into *Kevin Bridgeman & Others v. District Attorney for the Suffolk District & Others*, No. SJ-2014-0005 (Mass. Supreme Judicial Ct.).

In a January 2017 ruling in the *Bridgeman* case the SJC reviewed the effectiveness of the notice sent by the district attorneys. The Court determined "the notice sent by the district attorneys was wholly inadequate to provide the relevant Dookhan defendants with the information necessary to knowingly and voluntarily decide whether they should explore with counsel the possibility of withdrawing their plea or moving for a new trial."[27]

However, the Court rejected the defendant's remedy of a global order dismissing all Dookhan related cases. Instead the court ordered that the district attorneys file three letters with the Clerk of the Supreme Judicial Court within 90 days. The second of those letters was to identify all cases in their jurisdiction affected by Dookhan that "the District Attorney would move to vacate and dismiss with prejudice."[28]

---

[24] Source: http://www.boston.com/news/local/massachusetts/2013/11/22/annie-dookhan-former-state-chemist-who-mishandled-drug-evidence-agrees-plead-guilty/lhg1mwd9U3J8eh4tNBS63N/story.html
[25] Source: https://scholar.google.com/scholar_case?case=13900209628902371114&q=471+Mass.+465,+30+N.E.3d+806&hl=en&as_sdt=6,48
[26] Source: https://scholar.google.com/scholar_case?case=13900209628902371114&q=471+Mass.+465,+30+N.E.3d+806&hl=en&as_sdt=6,48
[27] Source: https://scholar.google.com/scholar_case?case=5928336817694206463&q=476+Mass.+298&hl=en&as_sdt=6,48
[28] Source: https://scholar.google.com/scholar_case?case=5928336817694206463&q=476+Mass.+298&hl=en&as_sdt=6,48

Those letters were filed by April 18, 2017. They identified a total of 21,587 convictions that the district attorneys in the seven counties thought warranted being vacated and the case dismissed. That was a little more than half of the more than 40,300 cases Dookhan "worked" on during her eight years as a chemist in the Hinton laboratory.

On April 19, 2017 Supreme Judicial Court Justice Frank M. Gaziano issued a Declaratory Judgment Order vacating the convictions in those 21,587 cases, and ordering their dismissal with prejudice. The Order stated:

> "... it is ORDERED that the convictions of G. L. c. 94C offenses that have been identified by the district attorneys in their respective second letters, as reproduced in Attachment A to this order, be and hereby are VACATED AND DISMISSED WITH PREJUDICE, and any outstanding warrants associated with those convictions are recalled."[29]

The Order effectively acquitted those 21,587 defendants because their cases can never be reprosecuted.

The April 19 Order attempted to shield the identity of the 21,587 exonerated people by impounding from public disclosure the district attorney's letters identifying them. However, only a day after the Order was issued, a letter was submitted to Justice Gaziano by Attorney Miriam Conrad that stated:

> "I am the Federal Public Defender for the Districts of Massachusetts, New Hampshire, and Rhode Island. My office represents indigent defendants charged with crimes in federal court. I write to request a copy of the list of defendants against whom charges were ordered dismissed by the Court on April 19, 2017, as well as any other lists the Court deems appropriate for my office to receive."[30]

Justice Gaziano has not yet responded to Conrad's request.

No information has been publicly disclosed about how many years the 21,587 defendants cumulatively spent wrongly imprisoned and/or on probation or parole.

The SJC's January 18, 2017 ruling in *Kevin Bridgeman & Others v. District Attorney for the Suffolk District & Others*, 476 Mass. 298 (1-18-2017) can be read at:
https://scholar.google.com/scholar_case?case=5928336817694206463&q=476+Mass.+298&hl=en&as_sdt=6,48

Investigation of Hinton Lab by the Massachusetts OIG

On November 5, 2012 Governor Patrick requested that the Massachusetts Office of the Inspector General ("OIG") investigate the Hinton Lab, that he had ordered shut down from drug testing on August 30, 2012. The OIG's report was released on March 4, 2014.[31] Key conclusions were:

- Dookhan was the sole bad actor at the Drug Lab.
- Management failures of lab directors contributed to Dookhan's ability to commit her acts of malfeasance.
- Department of Public Health ("DPH") Commissioner John Auerbach and his staff failed to respond appropriately to the report of Dookhan's breach of protocol.
- The Drug Lab lacked formal and uniform protocols with respect to many of its basic operations, including training, chain of custody and testing methods.
- The training of chemists at the Drug Lab was wholly inadequate.
- The Drug Lab failed to provide potentially exculpatory evidence to the parties in criminal cases by not disclosing information about additional, inconsistent testing results.
- The Drug Lab failed to uniformly and consistently use a valid statistical approach to estimate the weight of drugs in certain drug trafficking cases.
- The quality control system in place at the Drug Lab was ineffective in detecting malfeasance, incompetence and inaccurate results.

---

[29] Source: http://www.ma-appellatecourts.org/display_docket.php?dno=SJ-2014-0005
[30] Source: https://scholar.google.com/scholar_case?case=5928336817694206463&q=476+Mass.+298&hl=en&as_sdt=6,48
[31] Source: http://www.mass.gov/ig/publications/reports-and-recommendations/2014/investigation-of-the-drug-laboratory-at-the-william-a-hinton-state-laboratory-institute-20022012-executive-summary.html

- The security at the Drug Lab was insufficient in that management failed to appreciate the vulnerability of the drug safe, and did not do enough to protect its contents.
- There were no mechanisms in place to document discrepancies in chain-of-custody protocols or inconsistent testing results.

The report made a number of recommendations that it suggested could improve the quality control of drug handling and testing.

The OIG's March 4, 2014 report on the Investigation of the Drug Laboratory at the William A. Hinton State Laboratory Institute 2002–2012 can be read at, http://www.mass.gov/ig/publications/reports-and-recommendations/2014/investigation-of-the-drug-laboratory-at-the-william-a-hinton-state-laboratory-institute-2002-2012.pdf .

The Massachusetts legislature has appropriated $30 million for expenses related to the Dookhan scandal. However, wrongful imprisonment compensation lawsuits could significantly increase that amount.

Annie Dookhan's Eight Year Rampage Of Faking Scientific Evidence To Convict Innocent People Was Aided By The Legal System

Justice Denied Editorial*
May 11, 2017

Annie Dookhan's saga of sabotaging more than twenty-one thousand criminal cases in Massachusetts during the eight years she "worked" as a chemist in the Hinton State Laboratory is chronicled in *Justice Denied's* article, "21,587 People Exonerated In Massachusetts Due To Fraudulent Crime Lab Testing" (May 6, 2017).[32]

From her hiring in 2003 to her suspension in June 2011, Dookhan provided critical prosecution evidence by falsely certifying a suspected substance was an illegal drug. She was praised for her productivity and assistance to prosecutors during the years she was fabricating evidence by taking short-cuts and faking tests.

21,587 convictions in nine Massachusetts counties that depended on Dookhan's "drug certification" were vacated and the charges dismissed, on April 19, 2017 by the Massachusetts Supreme Judicial Court.

Justice Denied's article is the only known reporting about the Dookhan saga that makes the obvious observation she did not act alone: she was a cog in the law enforcement machine who was directly and indirectly assisted in her nefarious and illegal activities by hundreds, and possibly more than a thousand people. The success of her almost decade long subterfuge required willful blindness by a very large number of people intimately involved in Massachusetts' legal system: judges; prosecutors; defense lawyers; lab supervisors and technicians; and others.

It was only someone outside the legal system – her husband – who tried to alert authorities about Dookhan's dishonesty. However, his whistleblower warnings to the Norfolk County DA were ignored.

Given how deeply imbedded she was in the legal system, it isn't surprising that Dookhan's criminal career was only accidentally derailed: A lone person in the Hinton lab inadvertently noticed her slip-up of failing to provide initials in the evidence log book when she took out evidence without authorization in June 2011. If not for Dookhan's careless oversight, it is possible that to this day no one would be the wiser that she was engaging in her dirty work of framing ungodly numbers of innocent people.

Dookhan was the front person ... the "fall guy" for the consequences of what occurred during the eight years that scads of professional people believed on blind faith that she was a miracle worker at performing scientific tests for the Hinton Lab. She couldn't have done what she did without:

• The active assistance of her lab superiors and co-workers who didn't seriously question how she was able to perform tests at a superhuman rate;

• The support of prosecutors delighted that she reliably provided the evidence they needed to convict defendants;

• The lack of curiosity by a single judge about how a lone lab technician could provide evidence to convict an average of *11 people every court day* for year after year after year; and,

• The failure of a lawyer for a single one of the 21,587 exonerated defendants to question Dookhan's qualifications -- not even enough curiosity to do something as simple as checking her educational background and professional training to qualify as the expert who provided the evidence upon which their client's conviction was based. If only one defendant's lawyer had been competent enough to check Dookhan's background shortly after she was hired in 2003, her dishonesty would have been exposed and she would have been unceremoniously fired by the Hinton lab before she had the opportunity to reek havoc on the life of tens of thousands of people.

Dookhan was only able to do what she did because people in the Hinton lab, the seven prosecutors offices, the judges in the seven counties, and the public defenders and retained lawyers for the defendants, cooperated with

---

[32] "Annie Dookhan's Eight Year Rampage Of Faking Scientific Evidence To Convict Innocent People Was Aided By The Legal System," By Hans Sherrer, *Justice Denied*, May 11, 2017, online at, http://justicedenied.org/wordpress/?s=annie+dookhan .

her scam by effectively looking the other way in their assumption she was a super woman chemist -- and not a fraud.

Annie Dookhan took full advantage of the legal system's bureaucratic structure. The type of disinterested uncurious drones involved in the legal system's bureaucracy remains unchanged by the Dookhan scandal. It was an embarrassing episode that was a speed bump in business as usual.

The most important takeaway from Dookhan's eight-year rampage is there is very little to prevent innocent people from being preyed on by an unscrupulous person in a position of authority in any layer of the legal system.

Germany's Cabinet Approves Pardons For More Than 50,000 Men Convicted Of Homosexual Crimes

By Hans Sherrer
Justice Denied
March 27, 2017

Germany's cabinet has approved a bill that will pardon all men convicted after 1945 of a consensual homosexual crime. Men who are still alive will be granted compensation under the bill.[33]

Paragraph 175 of the German Criminal Code criminalized homosexual acts between males. The law was enacted in 1871, and it wasn't repealed until March 10, 1994. The law prohibited homosexual acts between males, both consensual and non-consensual. Although it was considered to be immoral and violate nature, lesbianism wasn't criminalized in Germany because it wasn't viewed as a threat to society.

The acts prohibited under Paragraph 175 were broadened in 1935 to include "lewd acts" by males, such as mutual masturbation and consensual touching. In 1950 the East German communist government repealed the 1935 amendments, while in West Germany they were confirmed by its Constitutional Courts.

East Germany repealed Paragraph 175 in 1968, but it was not repealed in West Germany. East and West Germany were unified in 1990, and four years later Germany repealed Paragraph 175.

More than 100,000 men were convicted of consensual homosexual acts under Paragraph 175 from 1871 to 1994. Around 60,000 men were convicted after the Federal Republic of Germany was created in May 1949.(The FRG was known as West Germany until it unified with East Germany in 1990, when it became known as Germany.)

Homosexual acts were vigorously prosecuted in West Germany under Paragraph 175. A judge in Frankfurt who presided over the conviction of more than 100 homosexuals in 1950 and 1951 said they were guilty of "degeneration" that was capable of "destroying the foundation of the state." In 1957 the German Supreme Court ruled that homosexuals imprisoned during the Nazi era were not eligible for compensation or a pension as Holocaust survivors because they had been lawfully imprisoned as criminals under Paragraph 175.

On March 22, 2017 Germany's cabinet approved a bill to make a legislative pardon available for all men convicted after 1948 of a consensual act under Paragraph 175. Men who are living can apply for a "vindication certificate" and relatives can apply for a posthumous pardon.

Under the bill men who are still living will be eligible for compensation of 3,000 Euros ($3,260), plus 1,500 Euros ($1,630) for each year in custody. For men granted a posthumous pardon, their compensation will not go to relatives, but to groups promoting homosexual rights. A Paragraph 175 conviction typically resulted in a two-year prison sentence.

The German government has set aside 30 million Euros ($32.6 million) to pay compensation claims.

Germany's Federal Minister of Justice and Consumer Protection Heiko Maas has been an advocate for the pardon and compensation bill: "The rehabilitation of men who ended up in court simply because of their homosexuality is long overdue. They were persecuted, punished and ostracised by the German state just because of their love for men, because of their sexual identity."

Men convicted of homosexual acts with children, or that involved violent or threatening behavior are excluded from rehabilitation and compensation under the bill.

The German parliament is expected to approve the rehabilitation bill that has broad support.

---

[33] "Germany's Cabinet Approves Pardons For More Than 50,000 Men Convicted Of Homosexual Crimes," By Hans Sherrer, *Justice Denied*, March 27, 2017, online at, http://justicedenied.org/wordpress/archives/3575 .

German Parliament Approves Pardoning Males Of Homosexual Convictions From 1945 To 1994

By Hans Sherrer
Justice Denied
justicedenied.org
June 26, 2017

Germany's lower house of parliament, the Bundestag, has overwhelmingly approved a bill that will vindicate all men who were convicted after May 8, 1945 to 1994 of a homosexual crime involving consensual relations between males 16 years or older.[1] The upper house of parliament has announced it will pass the bill.[34]

Men who are living can apply for a "vindication certificate," and relatives of men who are deceased can apply for a posthumous pardon.

The law can rehabilitate the reputation of upwards of 50,000 males.[2] An estimated 5,000 of them are still living, and they will be eligible for compensation of €3,000 Euros (US$3,372) for having been convicted, plus compensation of €1,500 Euros (US$1,686) for each year they were imprisoned.[3] A Paragraph 175 conviction typically resulted in a two-year prison sentence.

The German government has set aside 30 million Euros ($32.6 million) to pay compensation claims.

The families of males granted a posthumous pardon will not receive compensation.

[Addition to original article: The homosexual rehabilitation law went into effect on July 22, 2017. It is officially the "Act to Criminally Rehabilitate Persons Who Have Been Convicted of Performing Consensual Homosexual Acts After May 8, 1945, and to Amend the Income Tax Act, July 17, 2017. The law is in the: Bundesgesetzblatt [BGBl.] [Federal Law Gazette] I at 2443, BGBl website.]

History of German Criminal Code Paragraph 175

Paragraph 175 of the German Criminal Code criminalized homosexual acts between males. The law was enacted in 1871, and it wasn't repealed until March 10, 1994. The law criminalized all "sexual acts contrary to nature… be it between people of the male gender or between people and animals." Although lesbianism was considered to be immoral and violate nature, it wasn't criminalized in Germany because it wasn't viewed as a threat to society.

The acts prohibited under Paragraph 175 were broadened in 1935 to include "lewd acts" by males, such as mutual masturbation and consensual touching. In 1950 the East German communist government repealed the 1935 amendments, while in West Germany they were confirmed by its Constitutional Courts.

East Germany repealed Paragraph 175 in 1968, but it was not repealed in West Germany. East and West Germany were unified in 1990, and four years later Germany repealed Paragraph 175.

More than 100,000 men were convicted of consensual homosexual acts under Paragraph 175 from 1871 to 1994. An estimated 64,000 men were convicted of violating Paragraph 175 after the Federal Republic of Germany was created in May 1949. (The FRG was known as West Germany until it unified with East Germany in 1990, when it became known as Germany.)

Homosexual acts were vigorously prosecuted in West Germany under Paragraph 175. A judge in Frankfurt who presided over the conviction of more than 100 homosexuals in 1950 and 1951 said they were guilty of "degeneration" that was capable of "destroying the foundation of the state."

In 1957 the German Supreme Court ruled that homosexuals imprisoned during the Nazi era were not eligible

---

[34] "German Parliament Approves Vindicating Males Of Homosexual Convictions," By Hans Sherrer, *Justice Denied*, June 26, 2017, online at, http://justicedenied.org/wordpress/archives/3739 .

for compensation or a pension as Holocaust survivors because they had been lawfully imprisoned as criminals under Paragraph 175.

In 2002 the German Parliament approved a bill pardoning about 42,000 men convicted of a homosexual crime under Paragraph 175 during the Nazi era up to when the FRG was created in 1949.

Endnotes:

[1] Germany unconditionally surrendered on May 7, 1945, which ended the political rule of the National Socialist German Workers Party (NAZI's).

[2] An estimated 64,000 males were convicted of violating Paragraph 175 from 1949 to 1994, but the legislation only applies to convictions that didn't involve coercion or a male less than 16 years old.

[3] On June 21, 2017 the exchange rate was 1 EUR = 1.1241 USD

49,000 Men Posthumously Pardoned Of Homosexual Crimes In United Kingdom

By Hans Sherrer
Justice Denied
Feb. 3, 2017

The United Kingdom has posthumously pardoned about 49,000 males who were convicted of consensual homosexual activity that is no longer considered criminal. The pardons were included in the Policing and Crime Act 2017 that received Royal Assent on January 31, 2017. People still alive who were convicted of the affected crimes can apply for a pardon.[35]

The pardons were for males convicted of two crimes that have been partially decriminalized in the United Kingdom (England, Wales and Northern Ireland, with the exception of Scotland). Those crimes were:

- Buggery (sodomy/anal sex) was criminalized in 1533. The maximum penalty was death until 1861, when it was reduced to a maximum of life imprisonment.
- Gross Indecency was made a crime in the United Kingdom in 1885. It criminalized sexual activity other than sodomy between two males. The maximum penalty was two years in prison with or without hard labor.

The two crimes were decriminalized for private homosexual activity between consenting males over the age of 21 in England and Wales in 1967, in Northern Ireland in 1982 (and in Scotland in 1980). The age of consent for lawful homosexual activity was reduced to 18 in 1994. In 2000 it was reduced to 16 to equalize the age of consent for heterosexual and homosexual activity.

The movement for mass pardons arose after homosexual Alan Turing was granted a posthumous royal pardon by Queen Elizabeth II in 2013, for his conviction in 1952 for gross indecency with a 19-year-old male. Turing underwent "organo-therapy" – chemical castration – as an alternative to a prison sentence. He died in 1954 from what was ruled to be self-administered cyanide poisoning. Turing was an English mathematician, computer scientist, and cryptanalyst whose work breaking coded German military messages is credited with shortening World War Two.

The pardoning provision of the Policing and Crime Act 2017 is known as "Turing's Law."

Playwright Oscar Wilde was among the males posthumously pardoned on January 31st. Wilde was convicted in 1895 of gross indecency with a male, and sentenced to two years in prison at hard labor. Wilde died destitute in Paris in 1900.

The buggery pardons also apply to women because it was a non-gender specific crime. However, it isn't known if any women were actually convicted of buggery.

The pardons don't apply to convictions in Scotland, so the Scottish Parliament will have to separately deal with historic homosexual related prosecutions.

A summary of the UK's "Policing and Crime Act 2017" is online at,
https://www.gov.uk/government/collections/policing-and-crime-bill .

---

[35] "49,000 Men Posthumously Pardoned Of Homosexual Crimes In United Kingdom," By Hans Sherrer, *Justice Denied*, February 3, 2017, online at, http://justicedenied.org/wordpress/archives/3488 .

165 Men Cleared Of Historical Homosexual Convictions in England and Wales

By Hans Sherrer
Justice Denied
May 6, 2017

One-hundred-sixty-five men in England and Wales have had their historical conviction disregarded for a homosexual act that is no longer considered a crime.[36]

Homosexuality was decriminalized in 1967 in England and Wales. However, a conviction is still listed in court records and appears on a person's criminal record.

The Protection of Freedoms Act (PFA) enacted in 2012 by the United Kingdom's Parliament included a provision that allows a man convicted of a homosexual act that is no longer considered a crime to apply to the UK's Home Office for their conviction to be "disregarded."

The legislation primarily relates to two crimes involving actual sexual activity: buggery (anal sex) and gross indecency (oral sex, etc.). Minor activities such as holding hands with another male in public or going to a homosexual bar are not eligible to be disregarded.

The law applies to men convicted in England, Wales, and the British military. Most of the affected men were convicted under the Sexual Offences Act 1956, and corresponding offences under earlier legislation, and equivalent military offences.

To be eligible the homosexual activity underlying the conviction must have been consensual and with a person of 16 or over, and must not be a criminal offense under the Sexual Offences Act 2003. One of the crimes that doesn't qualify under the PFA is sexual activity in a public lavatory, which remains a criminal offense regardless of the participant's sex.

After a conviction is disregarded by the Home Office it is treated in official records as if it did not occur: it no longer appears on a person's criminal record; and, it is not admissible in court proceedings.

The Home Office's website has a webpage titled: "Statistics on disregards and pardons for historical gay sexual convictions."[37] The webpage was last updated January 2, 2018. The website lists that from October 1, 2012 to January 1, 2018, 165 men have had their conviction disregarded. The website lists the following statistics for "In scope applications":

Cases accepted:

16 = Buggery
145 = Gross Indecency
4 = Equivalent military offences
165 = Total

Cases rejected:

81 = Sexual activity in a public lavatory
8 = Non-consensual sex
7 = Other party under 16-years-old
96 = Total

The website lists that 268 applications were rejected for reasons such as they involved inapplicable crimes or convictions that occurred in Scotland or Northern Ireland. It is reported that the Scottish and Northern Ireland administrations intend to introduce their own legislation for the disregard of a historical homosexual conviction.

---

[36] "165 Men Cleared Of Historical Homosexual Convictions in England and Wales," By Hans Sherrer, *Justice Denied*, January 19, 2018, online at, http://justicedenied.org/wordpress/archives/4186 .

[37] The website is, https://www.gov.uk/government/uploads/system/uploads/attachment_data/file/118140/guidance-application.pdf .

Less than 2% of the estimated 16,000 men eligible to have a historical homosexual conviction disregarded have filed an application with the Home Office to do so.

The "Application Form & Guidance Notes for Applicants" to have a historical homosexual conviction in England and Wales disregarded. It costs no money to apply.

A man whose conviction is disregarded can also apply for a royal pardon. However, the Home Office's website doesn't state that a single person whose conviction was disregarded has in fact applied for a pardon.

On January 31, 2017 the United Kingdom posthumously pardoned about 49,000 males who were convicted of consensual homosexual activity that is no longer considered criminal.

www.ingramcontent.com/pod-product-compliance
Lightning Source LLC
Chambersburg PA
CBHW062234220526
45471CB00009B/3476